Intermittent Fasting 16/8

Complete Step-By-Step Guide to Lose Weight Quickly, Control Hunger and Feel Better Without Sacrificing Your Favorite Foods. Includes: Meal Plans with more than 70 Delicious Recipes.

By
Melany Flores

Contents

Introduction

I want to thank you and congratulate you for downloading the book, "Intermittent Fasting 16/8: Complete Step-By-Step Guide to Lose Weight Quickly, Control Hunger and Feel Better Without Sacrificing Your Favorite Foods. Included: Meal Plans with Delicious Recipes".

The 16:8 intermittent fasting has become so popular among people over the years. It is because of its many benefits that have helped many people. Intermittent has been shown to help people lose weight and also lower insulin levels and blood sugar. It also has many other benefits as you will find later in this book.

Intermittent is easy as opposed to what many people think that it is hard. There is little planning required and many individuals who practice it have said that they feel good generally and more energetic when fasting. When starting, it can be a bit hard, but you get used when the body has adapted.

Throughout this book, you will learn about the 16:8 method of intermittent fasting, how it works, and different foods you can use on this method. The book also has amazingly delicious recipes that are easy to prepare.

Thanks for choosing this book, make sure to leave a short review on Amazon if you enjoy it. I'd really love to hear your thoughts.

Enjoy reading!

Chapter 1:
Intermittent Fasting Explained

What is Intermittent Fasting?

Intermittent Fasting is an eating pattern where a person cycles between eating and fasting periods. Therefore, it is more of a way of eating than a diet.

How Intermittent Fasting Works

There is a lot of science behind why Intermittent Fasting works. Intermittent Fasting works because it restricts the body of toxins and allows itself to clear out any excess.

To know how Intermittent Fasting works, it is necessary that we start by understanding the difference between the fasted and fed state. When we eat, the body goes into a fed state whereby it is digesting and absorbing food. The fed state starts when you start eating and lasts for up to 3-5 hours when your body digests and absorbs the food that you just ate. At the fed state, it is very hard for the body to burn fat especially because your insulin levels are quite high (when you eat food, insulin is produced in response to

3

: the body cells to start absorbing the food from loodstream). At that time, the body's #1 priority is to use up the nutrients (mainly glucose) in your bloodstream. But as time goes on, the body then goes into a post-absorptive state- a fancy way of saying that the body is not processing food. This state lasts for about 8-12 hours after your last meal after which your body then goes into the fasted state. When your body is in the fasted state, it is likely to burn more fat because your insulin levels are quite low. At this state, your body can burn the fat that wasn't accessible during your fed state. Unfortunately, given that it takes about 12 hours after our last meal for our bodies to get into the fasted state, it is very rare for our bodies to get into this state. That's why many of us who start IF will lose fat pretty fast without even changing what we've been eating, how much you eat and how often you exercise. This is because fasting essentially puts your body into a fat-burning state, which you rarely make it to during your normal eating schedule.

The Benefits of Intermittent Fasting

Weight loss

Intermittent Fasting switches from periods of eating and to periods of fasting. If you fast, naturally your calorie intake will reduce, and it also helps you maintain your weight loss. It also prevents you from indulging in mindless eating. Whenever you eat something, your body converts the food into glucose and fat. It uses this glucose immediately and stores the fat for later use.

When you skip a few meals, your body starts to reach into its internal stores of fat to provide energy. As soon as the body begins burning fats due to the shortage of glucose, you will start to lose weight. Also, most of the fat that you lose is from the abdominal region. If you want a flat tummy, then this is the perfect diet for you.

Sleep

Lack of sleep is one of the main causes of obesity. When your body doesn't get enough sleep, the internal mechanism of burning fat suffers. Intermittent Fasting regulates your sleep cycle and, in turn, it makes your body effectively burn fats. A good sleep cycle has different physiological benefits - it makes you feel energetic and elevates your overall mood.

Resistance to illnesses

Intermittent Fasting helps in the growth and the regeneration of cells. Did you know that the human body has an internal mechanism that helps repair damaged cells? Intermittent Fasting helps kickstart this mechanism. It improves the overall functioning of all the cells in the body. So, it is directly responsible for improving your body's natural defense mechanism by increasing its resistance to diseases and illnesses.

A healthy heart

Intermittent Fasting assists in weight loss, and weight loss improves your cardiovascular health. A buildup of plaque in blood vessels is known as atherosclerosis. This is the primary cause of various cardiovascular diseases. The endothelium is the thin lining of blood vessels and any dysfunction in it results in atherosclerosis. Obesity is the primary problem that plagues humanity and is also the main reason for the increase of plaque deposits in the blood vessels. Stress and inflammation also increase the severity of this problem. Intermittent Fasting tackles the buildup of fat and helps tackle obesity. So, all you need to do is follow the simple protocols of Intermittent Fasting to improve your overall health.

A healthy gut

There are several millions of microorganisms present in your digestive system. These microorganisms help improve the overall functioning of your digestive system and are known as the gut microbiome. Intermittent Fasting enhances the health of these microbiomes and improves your digestive health. A healthy digestive system helps in better absorption of food and improves the functioning of your stomach.

Tackles diabetes

Diabetes is a significant threat on its own. It is also a primary indicator of the increase in risk factors of various cardiovascular diseases like heart attacks and strokes. When the glucose level increases alarmingly in the bloodstream and there isn't enough insulin to process this glucose, it causes diabetes. When your body resists insulin, it becomes difficult to regulate insulin levels in the body. Intermittent Fasting reduces insulin sensitivity and helps tackle diabetes.

Reduces inflammation

Whenever your body feels there is an internal problem, its natural defense is inflammation. It doesn't mean that all forms of inflammation are desirable. Inflammation can cause several serious health conditions like arthritis, atherosclerosis and other neurodegenerative disorders.

Any inflammation of this nature is known as chronic inflammation and is quite painful. Chronic inflammation can restrict your body's movements too. If you want to keep inflammation in check, then Intermittent Fasting will certainly come in handy.

Promotes cell repair

When you fast, the cells in your body start the process of waste removal. Waste removal means the breaking down of all dysfunctional cells and proteins and is known as autophagy. Autophagy offers protection against several degenerative diseases like Alzheimer's and cancer. You don't like accumulating garbage in your home, do you? Similarly, your body must not hold onto any unnecessary toxins. Autophagy is the body's way of getting rid of all things useless.

Higher Concentration and Brain Power

When subjected to food scarcity for a long time, mammals, including humans, will start to experience a decrease in their organ size. One of these organs is the brain. While some organs return to their original size over time, others may be impacted over the long term.

The brain handles the basic cognitive function of the body. In order to function properly and get the needed nutrients, it needs to return to its original size. However, if the brain becomes too foggy, getting the needed food nutrients will be pretty difficult, which might lead to malnutrition and even be fatal. However, during a shorter period of food scarcity, the brain becomes hyperactive in its search for food as a mechanism for survival.

Excessive availability of food and eating altogether makes us mentally dull. Reflect on a time when you were completely satisfied after a big meal. After eating a massive plate of food, you will likely go into a "food coma" and curl up and sleep, or maybe just watch your favorite TV show on Netflix rather than get the motivation to go achieve your goals. Without a doubt, satisfaction from food makes man naturally lose the drive to pursue his goals, which ultimately leads to dulling the brain. With this in mind, know that when you fast, your cognitive abilities are quickened. This improves your mental keenness, allowing you to achieve your health-related goals as opposed to excessively feeding.

It should be established here that there is no scientific research to support the notion that intermittent fasting alters mental alertness negatively. Fasting will not affect your cognitive function such as moods, mental alertness, reaction time, intention and sleep in any bad way. On the contrary, these things get boosted during fasting.

Fasting Promotes Autophagy and Protects Neurons

This is one of the many wondrous benefits of intermittent fasting which many people should look forward to. Fasting is amazing in that it keeps the brains cell from degeneration. This is because fasting prevents neural death.

Besides, fasting also triggers the process of autophagy in the brain – autophagy is the process in which the body gets rid of damaged body cells and brings out new ones. When the body is full of healthy, active and improved cells, it is strong and well-equipped to combat any diseases that might want to attack.

With autophagy, the risk of viral infection, as well as duplication of intracellular parasites, reduces drastically. This dramatically reduces intracellular pathogens, such as cancer cells. Besides, the brain and other body tissue cells are protected from abnormal growth, inflammation, and toxicity.

Reduced Risk of Depression

With intermittent fasting, there is an increase in the levels of a neurotransmitter called neurotrophic factor. When the body is deficient in this brain-derived factor, it contributes to significant issues such as depression and other mood disorders. Hence, intermittent fasting is really helpful in improving mental alertness and enhancing mood, which ultimately leads to a reduced tendency of developing these conditions.

There are a couple of metabolic features that get triggered when we fast that improve brain health. This explains why people who practice intermittent fasting do have lower levels of inflammation, low blood sugar levels, and reduced oxidative stress.

There are also indications that intermittent fasting can keep the brain protected against the risk of stroke.

Intermittent Fasting Fosters Immune Regulation

When you fast, part of the primary aim of the body is to keep the immune system healthy. This is why we encourage drinking a large quantity of water during the period of the intermittent fast, and afterward as well. Water can be spiced up with other detox agents which remove toxins from the digestive system and reduces the number of unhealthy gut microbes. Have in mind that the number of gut microbes present in the gastrointestinal tract is directly related to the immune system's function.

Intermittent fasting determines the number of inflammatory cytokines that the body has. Hence, it helps regulate the body's overall immune system. In the body, we have two significant cytokines which cause inflammation in the body: Interleukin-6 and Tumor Necrosis Factor Alpha. Fasting suppresses the release of these inflammatory pro-inflammatory cytokines.

Intermittent Fasting Reduces the Risk of Chronic Disease

People living with chronic autoimmune diseases like Crohn's disease, colitis, rheumatoid arthritis, and systemic lupus will definitely see remarkable improvement with intermittent fasting. The idea is simple. Fasting reduces the rate of an extreme inflammatory process in the bodies of these persons. With this, they have an ideal immune function.

For instance, cancer cells have between ten and seventy extra insulin receptors in contrast to healthy body cells. This happens as a result of the breakdown of sugar for fuel. With intermittent fasting, cancer cells are starved of sugar intake. This conditions the cells for damage through free radicals.

Improves Genetic Repair Mechanisms

The tendency of the body to live longer increases when it does not get enough food. This is because, with intermittent fasting, there is repair and regeneration of cells which comes about via a repair mechanism in the body. This is understandable, as the energy required for cell repair is lesser when compared to what is necessary for cell creation or division.

Hence, during the period of intermittent fasting, cell division and creation in the body becomes reduced. This is a necessary process, vital especially for the healing of malignant cells which thrive as a result of abnormal cell division.

In the body, the human growth hormone (HGH) takes care of the process of cell repair. It is a human growth hormone that brings about changes in metabolism that cause tissue repair and fat burning. Thus, when we fast, the body can concentrate more on repairing body tissues with amino acids and enzymes. This restores tissue collagen and also triggers an improvement in bones, ligaments, tendons and the general muscle function in the body.

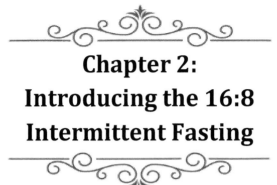

Chapter 2:
Introducing the 16:8
Intermittent Fasting

What is 16:8 Intermittent Fasting?

On this intermittent fasting method, you fast 16 hours of the day, and only eat during the remaining 8 hours of the day. The fasting window is a total of 16 hours a day; Your fasting window will mostly be during the time you are sleeping. During your fasting window, you will not eat any calories at all. Not eating when your mind and body are accustomed to eating will be difficult, but the challenge is mind over matter, and you matter, so you will succeed. Choose a time to start and stop your feeding window, when the feeding window stops, the fasting window starts, and when the fasting window stops, the feeding window starts, and so on.

People who cannot Fast on the 8:16 Plan

Intermittent Fasting can work for anyone. It can help anyone get healthy, lose weight and build lean muscles. However, there are a few exceptions. These exceptions are mainly for safety and health reasons. There are certain current health conditions that may worsen when you enter long fasting periods.

Sleep deprived or stressed

People who are experiencing high-stress levels for quite a long time are not good candidates for long fasting periods. These also include those who are sleep-deprived. Sleep deprivation and chronic high stress levels take a huge toll on health. Add fasting periods and the body will be subjected to extremely high strain. This can seriously deplete the body's capability to compensate and keep the organs working, further leading to a host of serious, potentially fatal conditions. There can be accelerated cell aging and death, accumulation of toxins, reduced immunity and slowing of metabolism and organ functioning.

It is advisable to address stress and sleep deprivation first before going in the IF lifestyle.

Sugar or food addict

If you have an addiction to sugar or certain food, fasting will become especially difficult. You will experience intensified cravings. If you are trying to wean off sugar, then fasting may cause you to relapse. There is a huge possibility that you will gorge on high sugar foods during the eating window. It is better to find other ways to deal with sugar addiction.

Medication

The actions of certain medications are affected by conditions in the body. Adjustments in dosages may be necessary. If you are taking medications for any health condition, inform your doctor about your plan in following the IF diet. Discuss with your doctor first before jumping into the IF life.

Pregnant and breastfeeding women, children

These people have high nutritional requirements for various metabolic and growth needs. Pregnant women need to eat to provide for the nutritional needs of the baby. Prolonged fasting states in pregnant women can lead to weakness and some potential complications like poor fetal growth.

For breastfeeding women, long fasting periods are also not recommended. They need to eat because they have to retain a good supply of nutrients for breast milk production. They also need the energy to replenish what they lost during the milk production process and the breastfeeding sessions. This stage can be really taxing on a woman's strength.

Children are at a stage of rapid growth and development. They have high nutritional requirements to fuel growth spurt and the maturation of their various organs. This is not the time to force their bodies into relying on fat stores during fasted states. It is still better for children to eat nutritious foods whenever they are hungry.

How the 16:8 IF diet works

In this method of IF, you only eat within 8 hours and then fast for 16 hours. Most people will think that this will cause them to experience extreme hunger. Normally, we eat all day - from the time we get up in the morning and until we finally go to sleep at night. That will be averaging anywhere from 12 to 14 hours. This is called the fed state.

In this state, the body focuses more on digesting and absorbing recently eaten foods. These processes can take up to several hours. During the fed state, the body's fat-burning processes are at a minimum. It is hard for the body to burn stored fats during the fed state because it relies on the energy derived from recent food consumption.

Insulin levels are high during the fed state. This is a response to the influx of glucose from foods. This more elevated insulin level also hinders fat burning.

After the fed state, the body enters the post-absorptive state. In this state, the body is neither digesting nor processing food. This usually lasts for about 1 to 2 hours after you last ate a meal.

After the post-absorptive state, if you still haven't eaten or drank anything that contains calories, your body enters the fasted state.

During the fasting period, your digestive system does not actively digest solid foods. Instead, it concentrates on fully metabolizing and absorbing the nutrients from foods. This becomes an opportunity to utilize foods fully and turn these into readily usable energy. This energy is quickly used up by the body. Efficient energy use lessens the possibility of converting excess calories into fats.

In the fasted state, levels of insulin are low. The inhibitory effect of insulin on fat-burning is reduced; hence, the body can turn on its fat burning processes at full force. This is why people who go on intermittent fasts burn fats and lose weight without changing their current diet. Even if they still eat the same kinds of foods every day, weight loss is evident.

Steady weight loss is achievable in the 8:16 intermittent fasting diet. This is because the cells burn glycogen stores for energy during the fasted state. When you eat again to break the fast, your body will turn energy into glycogen, instead of turning it into fat cells. This further enhances weight maintenance by reducing the amount of food that gets turned and stored as fats.

How to Follow The 16:8 Method

The 16:8 method is very flexible, and that means you can choose your own specific 8-hour eating window, according to your day. You might work shifts, and that means you sleep at different times. What you should do in that case is pick an 8-hour window which is when you are mostly awake. Obviously!

For example, if you are working nights and you are sleeping between the hours of 10am and 6pm, that means you can eat from 6pm until 2am. You would then probably be working until the following morning when you would head off to sleep, but you could drink coffee (unsweetened and black) to keep you going also, and plenty of water. This might not work for you, so you could think about shifting your pattern and starting it later, perhaps if you don't feel like eating the moment you open your eyes. You could then choose an eating window of 9pm and eat freely until 5am.

It's really up to you!

We've already covered the two main methods most people try with the 16:8, and that is the skipping breakfast and starting to eat at lunchtime routine, or in the case of someone who really needs breakfast because they can't concentrate without it.

It's not only about when you can eat, but it's also about what you eat too. Whilst there are no restrictions and no lists of foods you must eat and foods you shouldn't, always remember that if you suddenly pile a huge breakfast or lunch on your plate after fasting, you're going to end up with stomach ache. That could mean that you end up eating too many calories within your eating window and actually put weight on, or you end up with stomach disturbances for the rest of your eating window, don't get enough fuel during that time because your stomach is so bloated you can't bear to eat, and then you're hungry during your fasting time. It's about choosing carefully, which we'll talk about a little more shortly.

So, how many calories should you eat? It depends on whether you want to lose weight or maintain. A standard calorie amount to maintain weight is 2500 calories per day for a man and 2000 calories per day for a woman. This does depend on the height, current weight, and metabolism of the person, and is really only an average, healthy amount. If you want more solid guidelines on your specific circumstances, speak to your doctor, who will be able to give you a calorie aim plan tailored to your needs.

Within that calorie amount, you should make sure that you get a good, varied diet. That means proteins, carbs, fats, vitamins and minerals. Again, we're going to cover what you can and can't eat, loosely because there are no rules, shortly, but varied is the way to go. Ironically this will also help you enjoy your new lifestyle more, because you're not bored and eating the same things all the time. This is a pitfall many people suffer from regular low-calorie diets; the change is so restrictive that they end up eating the same thing day in, day out, and over time they get so bored and simply rebel against it. This usually ends in a binge day, which causes extreme guilt and then leads them to throw the diet in the bin and go back to eating whatever they want.

Whilst following the 16:8 method, you should also make sure that you drink plenty of water throughout the day, whether fasting or eating. This ensures that you don't become dehydrated and will also aid in digestion. In addition, you should also exercise too!

Now, there are no rules to say that you must exercise whilst following an intermittent fasting routine, but it will help you lose weight faster, and it will help with your general health and wellbeing. Exercise is fantastic on so many levels, not least helping to build lean muscle, which also boosts your ability to burn fat as an energy source. Exercise is also known to help with mental health issues, such as anxiety and depression, as well as stress. We all live stressful lives, and a little exercise can sometimes be enough to reduce it to levels which are extremely manageable. Aside from anything else, exercise can be a sociable and fun activity!

Chapter 3:
Foods to Enjoy/Avoid on 16:8

Foods to Eat

- Eggs - Make sure you eat the yolk because this contains the vitamins Nd protein!

- Leafy greens - We're talking about things like spinach, collards, Kale, and Swiss chards to name a few, and these are packed with fiber and low in calories too

- Oily and fatty fish, such as salmon - Salmon is a fish which will keep you feeling full, but it's also high in omega 3 fatty acids which are ideal for boosting brain health, reducing inflammation, and generally helping with weight loss too. If salmon isn't your bag, try mackerel, trout, herring, and sardines instead

- Cruciferous vegetables - In this case, you need to look toward Brussels sprouts, broccoli, cabbage, and cauliflower. Again, these types of vegetables contain a high fiber amount which helps you feel fuller for longer, but also have cancer-fighting attributes

- Lean meats - Stick to beef and chicken for the best options, but make sure that you go for the leanest cuts possible. You'll get a good protein boost here, but you can also make all manner of delicious dishes with both types of meat!

- Boiled potatoes - You might think that potatoes are bad for you, and in most cases, they are, especially if you fry them, but boiled potatoes are actually a good choice, especially if you lack in potassium. They are also very filling.

- Tuna - This is a different type of fish to the oily fish we mentioned earlier, and it's very low fat, but high in protein. Go for tuna which is canned containing water and not oil for the healthiest option. Pile it onto a jacket potato for a delicious and healthy meal!

- Beans and other types of legumes - These are the staple of any healthy diet and are super filling too. We're talking about things like kidney beans, lentils' Nd black beans here, and they're high in fiber and protein.

- Cottage cheese - If you're a cheese fan, there's no reason to deny yourself, but most cheeses are quite high in fat. In that case, why not opt for cottage cheese instead? This is high in protein and quite filling, but low in calories.

- Avocados - The fad food of the moment is actually very healthy and great for boosting your brain power! Mash it up on some toast for a great breakfast packed with potassium and plenty of fiber.

- Nuts - Instead of snacking on chocolate and crisps, why not snack on nuts? You'll get great amounts of healthy fats, as well as fiber and protein, and they're filling too. Don't eat too many, however, as they can be high in calories if you overindulge.

- Whole grains - Everyone knows that whole grains are packed with fiber and therefore keep you fuller for longer, so this is the ideal choice for anyone who is trying intermittent fasting. Try quinoa, brown rice, and oats to get you started.

- Fruits - Not all fruits are healthy, but they're certainly a better option than chocolate and crisps! You'll also get a plethora of different vitamins and minerals, as well as a boost of antioxidants into your diet - ideal for your immune system.

- Seeds - Again, just like nuts, seeds make a great snack, and they can be sprinkled on many foods, such as yogurt and porridge. Try chia seeds for a high fiber treat, whilst being low calorie at the same time.

- Coconut oil and extra virgin olive oil - You will no doubt have heard of the wonders of coconut oil, and this is a very healthy oil to try cooking with. Coconut oil is made up of something called medium-chain triglycerides, and whilst you might panic at the word triglycerides, these are actually the healthy type! If you want to go for something totally low in calories; however, then you can't beat extra virgin olive oil.

- Yogurt - Perfect for a gut health boost, yogurt is your friend because it will keep you full and it also has probiotic content, provided you go for products which say 'live and active cultures' on the pot. Avoid the overly sugary yogurt treats and anything which says 'low fat' normally isn't as positive as it sounds!

Foods to Avoid

- Sugary foods may curb your appetite, but they won't do anything good for your body in the long run. Steer clear for your future ease.

- Highly GMO foods are also things to avoid when you're working through your fast. They can offset the actual nutrition being provided by other foods in your diet.

Drinks to Take

You are allowed to take drinks while fasting. Go for drinks that are nutritious because they are good for the body. Some of the drinks that you can take are listed below;

Water with fruit or veggie slices will provide nourishment and flavor for those times when you're fasting and need a little extra boost!

Probiotic drinks like kombucha or kefir will work to heal your gut and tide you over till the next eating window.

Black coffee will become your new best friend but be sure not to add cream and sugar! They detract from the good work coffee can do for your body during IF.

Teas of any kind are soothing as well as healing for various elements of the body, mind, and soul. Once again, be sure to omit the cream and sugar!

Chilled or heated broths made from vegetables, bone, or animals can sustain one's energy during times of fast, too.

Apple Cider Vinegar shots are great for the tummy and for healing overall! Hippocrates' remedy for any ailment included this and a healthy regimen of fasting occasionally, so you're sure to succeed with this trick.

Water with salt can provide electrolytes, hydration, and brief sustenance for anyone whose stomachs won't stop grumbling.

Fresh-pressed juices are always great for the body, mind, and soul, and in times of IF, they can sustain one's energy and mood during day-long fast periods, in particular.

Wheatgrass shots are just as healthy as ACV shots, with a whole other subset of benefits. To awaken your body and give a jolt to your system, try these on for size.

Coconut water is more hydrating than standard water, and it's full of additional nutrients, too! Try this alternative if you need some enhancement to your usual water.

Chapter 4:
Other Types of Intermittent Fasting

Lean-Gains Method

This intermittent fasting method focuses on a healthy diet, fasting and rigorous exercises. It is popular because of its ability to convert fats straight to muscle. The main objective of this method is to fast 14-16 hours every day from when you wake up.

Waking up and fasting up to 1 pm and doing a warmup and stretches just before midday is a perfect approach to this method. From midday, do any exercise of choice for up to one hour and break your fast at 1 pm.

From there, go about your day's activities normally, and when it is around 4pm, eat again. Eat again at around 9 pm. This will give you about 15hours of fast until 1 pm on the following day. If it is challenging at the beginning, you can start fasting for 13 hours for several days and then increasing to 15 hours.

14:10 Method

In this method, you fast for 14 hours and eat during the other 100 hours. It works in a similar way as the 16:8. The difference is that the eating period in this method is 10 hours as opposed to 8 hours in 14:8. This allows more time for people whose routines are physically intense and also those who to eat later.

20:4 Method

Whereas 14:10 method was an easier step down from 16:8 method, 20:4 method is absolutely an increase in terms of difficulty. It's a more intense method certainly, for it requires 20 hours of fasting within each day with only a 4-hour eating window for the individual to gain all his or her nutrients and energy.

The majority of the people who opt to use this method end up having either one large meal with several snacks or they have two smaller meals with fewer snacks. 20:4 is flexible in that sense—the sense whereby the individual chooses how the eating window is divided amongst meals and snacks.

20:4 method is tricky, for many people instinctually over-eat during the eating window, but that's neither necessary nor is it healthy. People that choose 20:4 method should try to keep meal portions around the same size that they would normally have been without fasting. Experimenting on how many snacks are needed will be helpful as well with this method.

Many people end up working up to 20:4 from other methods, based on what their bodies can handle and what they're ready to attempt. Few start with 20:4, so if it's not working for you right away, please don't be too hard on yourself! Step it back to 16:8 and then see how soon you can get back to where you'd like to be.

The Warrior Method

The warrior method is quite similar to 20:4 method in that the individual fasts for 20 hours within each day and breaks fast for a 4-hour eating window. The difference is in the outlook and mindset of the practitioner, however. Essentially, the thought process behind the warrior method is that, in ancient times, the hunter coming home from stalking prey or the warrior coming home from battle would really only get one meal each day. One meal would have to provide sustenance for the rest of the day, recuperative energy from the ordeal, and sustainable energy for the future.

Therefore, practitioners of warrior method are encouraged to have one large meal when they breakfast, and that meal should be jam-packed with fats, proteins, and carbs for the rest of the day (and for the days ahead). Just like with 20:4 method, however, it can sometimes be too intense for practitioners, and it's very easy to scale this one back in forcefulness by making up a method like 18:6 or 17:7. If it's not working, don't force it to work past two weeks, but do try to make it through a week to see if it's your stubbornness or if it's just a mismatch with the method.

12:12 Method

12:12 method is a little easier, along with the lines of 14:10, rather than 16:8 or 20:4. Beginners to Intermittent Fasting would do well to try this one right off the bat. Some people get 12 hours of sleep each night and can easily wake up from the fasting period, ready to engage with the eating window. Many people use this method in their lives without even knowing it.

To go about 12:12 method in your life, however, you'll want to be as purposeful about it as you can be. Make sure to be strict about your 12-hour cut-offs. Make sure it's working and feeling good in your body, and then you're invited to take things up a notch and try, say, 14:10 or maybe your own invention, like 15:11. As always, start with what works and then move up (or down) to what feels right (and even possibly better).

5:2 Method

5:2 method is popular among those who want to take things up a notch generally. Instead of fasting and eating within each day, these individuals take up a practice of fasting two whole days out of the week. The other 5 days are free to eat, exercise, or diet as desired, but those other two days (which can be consecutive or scattered throughout the week) must be strictly fasting days.

For those fasting days, it's not as if the individual can't eat anything altogether, however. In actuality, one is allowed to consume no more than 500 calories each day for this Intermittent Fasting method. I suppose these fasting days would be better referred to as "restricted-intake" days, for that is a more accurate description.

5:2 method is extremely rewarding, but it is also one of the more difficult ones to attempt. If you're having issues with this method, don't be afraid to experiment the next week with a method like 14:10 or 16:8, where you're fasting and eating within each day. If that works better for you, don't be ashamed to embrace it! However, if you're dedicated to having days "on" and days "off" with fasting and eating, there are other alternatives, too.

Eat-Stop-Eat (24-Hour) Method

The eat-stop-eat or 24-hour method is another option for people who want to have days "on" and "off" between fasting and eating. It's a little less intense than the 5:2 method, and it's much more flexible for the person, depending on what he or she needs. For instance, if you need a literal 24-hour fast each week and that's it, you can do that. Meanwhile, if you want a more flexible 5:2 method-type thing to happen, you can work with what you want and create a method surrounding those desires and goals.

The most successful approaches to the eat-stop-eat method have involved more strict dieting (or at the very least, cautious and healthy eating) during the 5 or 6 days when the individual engages in the week's free-eating window. For the individual to truly see success with weight loss, there will have to be some caloric restriction (or high nutrition focus) those 5 or 6 days, too, so that the body will have a version of consistency in health and nutrition content.

On the one or two days each week the individual decides to fast, there can still be highly-restricted caloric intake. As with the 5:2 method, he or she can consume no more than 500 calories worth of food and drink during these fasting days so that the body can maintain energy flow and more.

If the individual engages in exercise, those workout days should absolutely be reserved for the 5 or 6 free-eating days. The same goes for the 5:2 method. Try not to exercise (at least not excessively) on those days that are chosen for fasting. Your body will not appreciate the added stress when you're taking in so few calories. As always, you can choose to move up from eat-stop-eat to another method if this works easily and you're interested in something more. Furthermore, you can start with a strict 24-hour method and then move up to a more flexible eat-stop-eat approach! Do what feels right, and never be afraid to troubleshoot one method for the sake of choosing another.

Alternate-Day Method

The alternate-day method is similar to eat-stop-eat and 5:2 methods because it focuses on individual days "on" and "off" for fasting and eating. The difference for this method, in particular, is that it ends up being at least 2 days a week fasting, and sometimes, it can be as many as 4.

Some people follow very strict approaches to alternate-day method and literally fast every other day, only consuming 500 calories or less on those days designated for fasting. Some people, on the other hand, are much more flexible, and they tend to go for two days eating, one day fasting, two days eating, one day fasting, etc. The alternate-day method is even more flexible than eat-stop-eat in that sense, for it allows the individual to choose how he or she alternates between eating and fasting, based on what works for the body and mind the best.

The alternate-day method is like a step up from eat-stop-eat and 24-hour methods, especially if the individual truly alternates one-day fasting and the next day eating, etc. This more intense style of fasting works particularly well for people who are working on equally intense fitness regimens, surprisingly. People who are eating more calories a day than 2000 (which is true for a lot of bodybuilders and fitness buffs) will have more to gain from the alternate-day method, for you only have to cut back your eating on fasting days to about 25% of your standard caloric intake. Therefore, those fasting days can still provide solid nutritional support for fitness experts while helping them sculpt their bodies and maintain a new level of health.

Spontaneous Skipping Method

Alternate-day method and eat-stop-eat method are certainly flexible in their approaches to when the individual fasts and when he or she eats. However, none of those mentioned above plans are quite as flexible as spontaneous skipping method. Spontaneous skipping method literally only requires that the individual skip meals within each day, whenever desired (and when it's sensed that the body can handle it).

Many people with more sensitive digestive systems or who practice more intense fitness regimens will start their experiences with IF through spontaneous skipping method before moving on to something more intensive. People who have very haphazard daily schedules or people who are around food a lot but forget to eat will benefit from this method, for it works well with chaotic schedules and unplanned energies.

Despite that chaotic and unorganized potential, spontaneous skipping method can also be more structured and organized, depending on what you make of it! For instance, someone desiring more structure can choose which meal each day they'd like to skip. Let's say he chooses to skip breakfast each day. Then, his spontaneous skipping method will be structured around making sure to skip breakfast (a.k.a.—not to eat until at least 12 pm) daily. Whatever you need to do to make this method work, try it! This method is made for experimentation and adventurousness.

Crescendo Method

The method is very well-suited for female practitioners (since their anatomies can be so detrimentally sensitive to high-intensity fasts). Essentially, this approach is made for internal awareness, gentle introductions, and gradual additions, depending on what works and what doesn't. It's a very active, trial-and-error type of method.

Through crescendo method, the individual starts by only fasting 2 or 3 days a week, and on those fast days, it wouldn't be a very intense fast at all. In fact, it wouldn't even be so strict that the individual would have to consume no more than 500 calories, like with 5:2, eat-stop-eat, and others. Instead, these "fasting" days would be trial periods for methods like 12:12, 14:10, 16:8, or 20:4. The remaining 4 or 5 days out of the week would be open eating-window periods, but again, the practitioner is encouraged to maintain a healthy diet throughout the week.

Crescendo method works extremely well for female practitioners because it enables them to see how methods like 14:10 or 12:12 will affect their bodies without tying them to the method hook, line, and sinker. It allows them to see what each method does to their hormone levels, their menstruation tendencies, and their mood swings. Therefore, the crescendo method encourages these people to be more in touch with their bodies before moving too quickly into something that could do serious anatomical and hormonal damage.

Crescendo method will work extremely well for overweight or diabetic practitioners, too, for it will allow them to have these same "trial period" moments with all the methods before choosing what feels and works best, based on each individual situation.

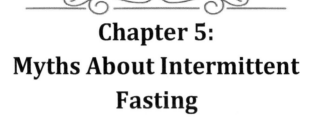

Chapter 5:
Myths About Intermittent Fasting

*T*here are many myths out there about Intermittent Fasting. the common myths are as follows;

MYTH: Your body will definitely enter in starvation mode.

TRUTH: Your body will not definitely enter in starvation mode through Intermittent Fasting. Skipping meals or adjusting to longer periods between meals where you don't eat is not going to make you starve. It's going to help your body remember how to absorb nutrients. It's going to help you thrive instead.

MYTH: You'll lose muscle in this endeavor.

TRUTH: This myth goes along the same lines as the first one, above. Just like your body won't enter the starvation mode (unless something goes very, very wrong or you're trying to do too much); your body won't lose muscle through IF. The only reason why intermittent fasting would cause muscle loss would be if it was causing you to starve, but once again, the first myth addresses this falsity, making this myth false as well.

MYTH: You'll almost assuredly overeat during eating windows, and that's not healthy at all.

TRUTH: While some people will have the instinct to overeat during eating windows, not everyone will overeat. Even those who do at the start will realize how to move forward without this overeating instinct in the future. Your body will urge you to overeat because, at the start, it won't realize what you're doing to it, but as long as you keep portion sizes largely the same and don't gorge on snacks, your body will adjust and so will your appetite.

MYTH: Your metabolism will slow down dangerously.

TRUTH: Your metabolism won't slow down just because you're eating less often. People who think this myth is true, only assume that restricted caloric intake will make one's metabolism slow down over time, but these individuals forget that IF isn't necessarily about cutting down calories overall. It's actually about cutting down the times during which one consumes calories. There needn't be any caloric restriction whatsoever! It just depends on the practitioner and what he or she decides to do with dieting in addition to IF.

MYTH: You'll only gain weight if you try skipping meals.

TRUTH: This myth is based on the same logic that drives the myth about overeating. If you gorge yourself during your eating windows, you'll surely gain weight, but hardly anyone will continuously gorge with IF. Anyone who tries will realize how unsuccessful it is, so he or she will not continuously gorge in response. Anyone who doesn't realize his or her efforts with eating are unsuccessful will soon realize that something's wrong, as his or her weight shows no improvement. Skipping meals never necessarily means that someone will gain weight. It just means that people who skip meals and gorge or overeat when it is mealtime won't see the desired effects.

MYTH: During fast periods, you literally can't eat anything.

TRUTH: This myth is partially true and partially false. It's true only for methods like 12:12, 14:10, 16:8, and 20:4 that require fasting and eating in alternation within each individual day. For 12:12 method, for example, you'd spend 12 hours fasting and 12 hours eating. In this case, you would definitely not eat anything or consume any calories during that 12-hour fasting window, but the same isn't true for methods that alternate between days "on" and days "off" between fasting and eating. For those types of methods, you absolutely can eat during fasting periods! It might feel counterintuitive as you read these words, but you don't explicitly have to eat nothing during fast periods. Most methods that have full days of fasting actually allow for caloric intake as long as it's restricted by 20-25% of one's normal intake. Therefore, for methods like 5:2, alternate-day, eat-stop-eat, and crescendo, on days when you're fasting, you can still consume around 500 calories, and that will help a lot!

MYTH: There's only one way to do IF that's right and truly the best.

TRUTH: This myth is absolutely and utterly false. There is no one right way to practice Intermittent Fasting, and part of the beauty of IF is that there are so many different methods, meaning each approaching IF likely has a few different options to choose from. Similarly, different body and personality types will be drawn to different methods, based on individuals' abilities and goals. IF is about flexibility, adjustment, and self-correction. There's no one right method for everyone, and there's no "best" method to strive for. Do whatever method feels right and suits your life, and once you've found it, practice it as long as you can! That's far more realistic and accessible.

MYTH: It's not natural to fast like that.

TRUTH: It's more natural to practice Intermittent Fasting than it is to eat three full meals each day! It's more connected to our evolutionary drives and to our primitive selves to eat like this. And it's better for our brains, hearts, cells, and digestive systems to have a break from food once in a while to recalibrate. As you learned in the Introduction, people have been practicing Intermittent Fasting as long as humans have been in existence. It's only myths like this that circulate today that make it seem like IF is foreign, unhealthy, and dangerous. Animals of all types become healthier after periods of fasting, and humans are no different. Remember that we are animals and that IF is in our nature. Proceed with that confidence and knowledge!

Chapter 5:
Frequently Asked Questions

*M*ost types of changes come with a lot of questions and intermittent fasting is no different. Here are some frequently asked questions from beginners.

Can I have coffee?

Yes, you can have black coffee, water, and plain steeped tea.

Can I add cream/sugar/milk in my coffee?

The goal of fasting is not to add calories, so the answer is no, you should not add anything to your coffee. However, I have heard of cases in which intermittent fasters add less than 50 calories to their coffee and they have claimed to still be successful with intermittent fasting; I have heard that it does not affect their fasted state, but keep in mind all individuals are not created equal. I would not recommend adding anything to your coffee, but if adding something to your coffee still makes this a good change for the goal you have for yourself, then give it a try.

Does intermittent fasting work well with veganism, paleo, keto, vegetarianism, or any other styles of eating?

Yes, the beauty of intermittent fasting is that it can be combined with any style of eating unless otherwise directed by a medical professional. You can turn your style of eating into the 16:8 method with ease, as this change does not restrict or state the style/types of food you eat, it is specifically based on the timing of your eating.

Is there an alternative to the 16:8 method if I cannot initially fast 16 hours and raise it up to 16?

Yes, especially for women, it is recommended that if women cannot or are not willing to do a 16 hour fast, they can start with a 14-hour fasting window and 10-hour feeding window. This is recommended for women, but men can start here if needed. Once the 14 hours is mastered, you can then work your way up to the 16:8 method.

Can I have a cheat meal?

Technically, you can eat what you want when intermittent fasting; there are no food group restrictions. There is no cheat meal to have, unless you have decided that you have put yourself on some type of restrictive meals/foods to not indulge in, if so, then yes, but I recommend to always eat in moderation.

What are some healthy snack foods to eat on the go during my feeding window?

Pepperoni slices, fruit, veggie tray, Skinny Pop popcorn individual bags (unless you will always measure the servings before consuming), turkey/beef jerky, individual peanut butter cups, whole grain cereal, almond milk, eggs, rice cakes, nuts (individual bags), hummus, and more.

I am too hungry during my fasting window. What should I do?

Be patient and your body to adapt to this change. This may take some time, for some, it occurs fast, for others, it may take a week or so, but this depends on how you were eating before you began this lifestyle. According to Collier in 2013, your body is still adjusting to how it was functioning before and is fighting you to get back to that way, as most people were eating more frequently and maybe even more meals or snacks during the day. Eventually, you will not feel this way. Eventually, you will adapt to your feeding and fasting windows and the urge to eat or the thought of starving will get easier and easier until it goes away.

Why am I not losing fat faster, like other people are?

It is more than likely a combination of not eating the appropriate portions when you are eating and/or not preparing to eat the right food choices. Although fat and weight loss can still happen, it is more frequent and visible when the appropriate food choices and portions are selected and prepared.

How can I stay full longer?

Eat more fiber and drink more water, stay hydrated.

Do I have to eat low carb?

No, you can eat what you want during your feeding window. I recommend eating proportionately and choosing healthier food options. Instead of white bread choose whole grain bread. Instead of white rice choose brown rice. Instead of anything with high fructose corn syrup, scratch it off, instead of canned fruit, eat fresh fruit.

Should I exercise in the fasted state?

You can, but it is not required. It is also not recommended on heavy lifting days.

What if I am on medications and must eat with my morning medications?

In this case, you would need to make your feeding window begin at whatever time you take your meds. I would recommend taking your meds as late as you can in the mornings but do get authorization of your plan from a medical professional.

Should I discuss this with my medical professional before beginning the change?

Yes, you should always discuss diet changes with a medical professional before you begin.

Frequent mistakes

People have failed due to the following frequent mistakes. Don't be one of these people, be knowledgeable and plan and think ahead.

One of the biggest mistakes beginners make is not finishing this book to the end and not taking this information seriously; basically, starting too soon, before you are prepared to start. While reading this book, it's a good idea to take notes, and jot down an individual plan while reading and sometimes doing further research during your reading. It wouldn't hurt even to read this book twice, especially if this is your first exposure to fasting, specifically intermittent fasting.

Another mistake that is made, not only with intermittent fasting but with any and most diet plans or lifestyle eating changes, is when people try to implement too many changes at once. Becoming a vegan and implementing intermittent fasting at the same time is not a great idea. Starting to work out with a trainer 4 days a week and implement intermittent fasting is not recommended. It is not goodstarting a new job with varying schedules and implement intermittent fasting at the same time. It is also nota good idea starting a new medication, a new workout plan, and intermittent fasting at the same time. Not to say this is impossible, it is, but on average these are too many changes at once for a beginner.

Most of us have been taught to eat 3 good sized meals a day, breakfast, lunch, and dinner (which includes dessert) and to have snacks in between meals, so anything outside of this set up seems out of the norm. Many people are habituated to always eating something during most times of their day. Most events we host or attend, are surrounded by food and beverages, so food is always readily available. Being without food for 16 hours sounds foreign and impossible because it is not what we are accustomed too.

Intermittent fasting brings about a new idea that life is not all about eating food all the time. People are in fear of this idea at the start, which denotes negativity; they may fail in making this big of a change due to their own negative assumptions and thoughts. Do not be afraid to be hungry; you will not starve during these 16 hours, you will survive, and be successful with weight loss, better health, and weight management.

During the beginning stages of intermittent fasting, it is vital to NOT constantly watch the clock. It is recommended that you use your time wisely. Intermittent fasting will inadvertently assist you with your time management if you listen to this recommendation. While fasting, be productive, stay busy, because 16 hours of fasting is just that 16 hours of not eating. Most people will sleep the majority of the 16 hours of fasting times, but it will take time for your body AND your mind to become accustomed to not eating breakfast or not eating or drinking whatever as soon as you wake up each morning, so make sure you attempt to stay busy and never get too much in your heard or get bored.

Some people are familiar with eating mostly junk foods: no nutrients, minerals, vitamins, or any form of a balanced meal. Sugar cravings, addictions, and food obsessiveness for these people will be one of your hardest challenges. A good way to counterbalance this is not to purchase sugary, unhealthy foods to be stored near you, especially during the beginning stages of intermittent fasting. We are accustomed to snacking all the time, snacking is allowed during the feeding windows, but it is recommended to make better snack options, choose fruit, not donuts, choose whole grain cereal instead of Frosted Flakes, choose nuts over candy bars.

Your body needs to be always hydrated. Sometimes your body sends your brain signals that it's hungry when you are not physically hungry; you are instead thirsty and needing liquid intake. A major mistake is not drinking an adequate amount of water daily. To assist with making water intake routine, people can start each meal with an 8 oz glass of water, drink steeped tea during either fasting or feeding times (both are acceptable), start the morning with a glass of lemon water, and/or during the feeding windows infuse water with fruits, mints, and more.

Lastly, but in no way least of the mistakes made by beginners is the idea that you don't need to choose your foods wisely. Yes, you can eat your favorite foods, yes you can still eat out at restaurants with your families, yes you can still attend social events which includes a buffet and more, but it is recommended to choose healthier options, use portion control, and read food labels if possible; basically, make smart choices to ensure you have optimal results while intermittent fasting. There is no diet or way of eating in which you can lose weight or maintain weight with no regard to calorie intake.Calories count no matter what diet or way of eating you are following. Intermittent fasting is no different; you cannot get away with excessive calorie intake.

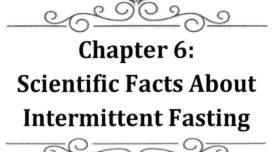

Chapter 6:
Scientific Facts About
Intermittent Fasting

Intermittent fasting has been found to help people lose weight and also promote their health. However, conventional calorie restrictions diets are superior to IF. This is according to a study called *HELENA-*intermittent fasting's largest research in history. It was done by scientists from Heidelberg University Hospital and the German Cancer Research Center (DKFZ). They found out that there are different routes to achieve a healthier weight. You just have to get a diet plan that suits you best.

Increased Brain Cell Production

This is one of the most surprising yet amazing benefits of intermittent fasting. Fasting has been shown to enhance neurogenesis, which is the process of developing new brain cells and nerves. Optimizing the brain's neurogenesis can help to improve your mood, focus, memory, and other cognitive functions.

In fact, one study published in the Journal of Cerebral Blood Flood and Metabolism shows that mice that fasted produced more brain cells than mice on a regular diet. The researchers measured cell production, cell death, and neurogenesis. Following 3 months of intermittent fasting, the mice that fasted showed an increase in brain cells and had less brain cell damage from a stroke.

Another study, *Chronic Intermittent Fasting Improves Cognitive Functions and Brain Structures in Mice*, by Liaoliao Li, Zhi Wang, and ZhiyiZuo showed that intermittent fasting leads to improvements in brain activity and cognitive functions in mice. 7-week old mice were either put on an alternate-day fasting or a high-fat diet for 11 months. There was a substantial difference between the two groups. Mice on the alternate day fasting diet had higher levels of learning and memory, more cell production in the brain, and lower levels of oxidative stress. In comparison, mice on the high-fat diet were obese with hyperlipidemia and had poor exercise tolerance and performance.

Research shows that fasting may have a similar positive effect on your brain as exercise has on your body. Both of these activities place stress on the brain, making it stronger and more resistant to stressful stimuli. The brain reacts to stressful stimuli by building up new neurons and connections.

Both exercise and fasting seem to boost ketones and mitochondria production within the brain. In addition, new neural connections and synapses are created and strengthened. This leads to better memory and learning.

Increased BDNF production

Besides promoting neurogenesis, fasting increases brain-derived neurotrophic factor (BDNF). BDNF is a growth factor and is critical for cognitive function. BDNF produces new brain cells and nerves and creates connections between them. It also helps with learning and memory and is a natural antidepressant. Higher levels of BDNF keep neurons healthy and ensures the neurons communicate effectively with one another. In contrast, lower levels of BDNF can increase the risks of memory loss, dementia, and other cognitive problems.

According to a study by Bronwen Martin, Mark P. Mattson, and Stuart Maudsley (2006), fasting for 16 to 18 hours can increase BDNF production by as much as 100 percent, and fasting for 36 hours can increase BDNF production by as much 400 percent.

Other research by the National Institute on Aging in the U.S. has shown that mice who fasted every other day showed improvements in their cognitive functioning. The team of researchers put 40 mice on an alternate day fasting schedule (one day on, one day off) and noted that the parts of their brain responsible for memory were more active.

In addition, the brain protein, brain-derived neurotrophic factor (BDNF), increased by up to 50 percent in the mice that fasted.

May protect against Alzheimer's

Alzheimer's is a dementia type that slowly destroys memory and mental functions over time. Currently, there isn't a cure for Alzheimer's. One study looked at whether intermittent fasting improved the cognitive function of people with Alzheimer's. Researchers looked at ten people with early signs of Alzheimer's. Each person was asked to make a number of lifestyle modifications, including fasting for 12 hours each night. 6 months later, 9 out of the 10 subjects showed improvements in their cognitive abilities.

How Intermittent fasting impacts human growth hormone (HGH))

When you fast, your HGH levels go up. This helps to preserve lean muscle and breaks down fat. When free fatty acids are released and converted into energy, this process is known as lipolysis. Obese individuals generally have inefficient lipolysis processes. Lower HGH levels may be one possible cause of this.

Besides fasting, HGH levels can also be increased by exercise. These levels can fluctuate throughout the day since the pituitary gland releases HGH hormone in spurts. Our HGH levels are generally higher when we wake up. We produce growth hormone during sleep, which increases our blood glucose that can be used as fuel for the day. Thus, this idea that you have to eat breakfast to get energy is false. Your body is already primed and ready to function in the morning without having to load up on food.

In addition, many popular breakfast choices, such as cereals and toasts, are high in sugar and carbs. This can make you feel tired andlethargic.

HGH is a natural testosterone booster and has been shown to increase muscle strength and improve exercise performance. In fact, many bodybuilders and athletes may inject additional HGH to improve their performance. A study by the International Journal of Endocrinology looked at the effects of HGH on muscle strength in men over 50 years old. 14 healthy male subjects were divided into two groups: seven subjects were placed in the HGH therapy group, while the remaining seven were placed in the placebo group. 6 months later, all the participants were tested for their body composition and muscle strength, including a number of exercises, such as the leg press and bench press exercises. The HGH group showed a significant increase in muscle strength in the lower body compared to the placebo group.

One study by the Journal of Clinical Investigation showed that intermittent fasting dramatically increased the growth hormone production in men.

Another research from the Journal of Clinical Endocrinology and Metabolism showed that intermittent fasting reduced leptin levels in obese adults. This led to instantaneous increases in testosterone levels.

A fascinating study by the European Journal of Endocrinology showed that fasting dramatically increased the Gonadotropin-Releasing Hormone

(GnRH), a testosterone precursor, in both obese and non-obese men. The researchers looked at 17 men who were divided into two groups (9 men in the obese group and 8 men in the non-obese group). GnRH levels in the obese men rose by 26% while the GnRH levels in non-obese men rose by 67%. In addition, serum testosterone levels shot up by 180% in those in the non-obese group.

Fasting and Leptin

Fasting is one way to increase leptin and glucose sensitivity. Leptin levels have been shown to fall after a short-term fast and return back to normal after eating. Any form of fasting should work since it forces the body to burn through excess glucose stores.

A study published in the Journal of Clinical Endocrinology & Metabolism looked at how fasting affected leptin levels in nine obese men. After three days of fasting, the researchers noted that the subjects had reductions in total body mass ($21.4 \pm 3.7\%$) and leptin ($76.3 \pm 8.1\%$). Leptin levels returned to baseline levels within 12 hours of eating.

Another study published in Metabolism looked at the changes in serum leptin and endocrine in both men and women after 7 days of fasting. The subjects were made up of 11 men and 13 women. After 7 days of fasting, the researchers noted that both men and women lost an average of 4 percent in body weight. Leptin decreased in both men (from 3.7 ± 0.5 to 2.1 ± 0.4 ng/mL) and women (16.2 ± 1.9 ng/mL to 6.0 ± 0.8 ng/mL) following fasting. Compared to men, women had higher levels of leptin before and after calorie restriction. However, women showed a bigger decrease in leptin levels overall.

As these studies show, fasting seems to be effective at reducing leptin levels and body mass in both men and women.

Fasting and Inflammation?

There is proof that intermittent fasting may be an effective way to reduce inflammation. Research shows that intermittent fasting may have a protective effect against high blood pressure, high insulin and inflammation. There is also evidence that shows fasting may help with type 2 diabetes and autoimmune conditions like MS and rheumatoid arthritis.

In a study published by the National Center for Biotechnology Information, researchers fed mice either a low-fat or high-fat diet for 10-12 weeks. After fasting, the mice fed a low-fat diet lost more body weight (18% compared to 5%), performed better on memory and learning tasks, and showed better locomotor activity compared to the mice on a high-fat diet. Low-fat mice also had an improved nervous system and immune function. The researchers concluded that fasting has an anti-inflammatory effect on the neuroimmune system, which a high-fat diet prevents.

Ramadan fasting has been shown to have a positive effect on reducing inflammation and may even help to treat fatty liver. One study published in the US National

Library of Medicine in 2017 compared 83 people with Nonalcoholic fatty liver disease (NAFLD), 42 who fasted and 41 controls who didn't fast for Ramadan. Those who fasted showed significant reductions in glucose, plasma insulin, insulin resistance, and inflammation compared to the nonfasting group.

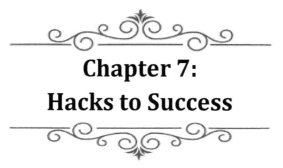

Chapter 7:
Hacks to Success

There are many principal tips and tricks that I use till this day to continue to ensure my success. While intermittent fasting is all about the timing of your meals and fasting, it can be so much more if you decide to use all the resources available to you to keep it exciting, continue to learn new things, be creative, be consistent and prepare and be always prepared. Intermittent fasting along with the hacks discussed below will change your weight and your life forever.

Sharing is Caring

I am not certain if this will help anyone other than myself or not, but it did help and is still helping me. I have learned that I am best at all things in life when I am helping others along the way. I have always shared my knowledge with people day in and day and have become a coach of intermittent fasting to many. By encouraging others, I have simultaneously helped myself, because it's a shame to teach what you can't follow right? I won't be that type of coach. I practice what I am teaching. Me writing this book has helped me learn that I know so much about this topic, which is why I have been so much more successful this time around.

Apps to Download

Pinterest is such a good resource to use when it comes to planning meals to keep eating the healthier way. This app includes links to recipes, grocery lists, meal idea, how to prep these meals, and more. YouTube, of course, is a great resource to review other people's struggles, peaks, and pits, before and after pictures, to hear their stories, to help you stay motivated and understand that most of what you go through while attempting to make this a habit, others have gone through the same things. MyFitnessPal's blog and community sections of its app is another great resource to use to join communities that are specific to intermittent fasting and all its components

These are good apps to have downloaded on your mobile device, iPad, or tablet. Using all your free time on these apps should be your new hobby instead of scrolling on your social media, especially since everything you see and hear will contribute to the success of making intermittent fasting a hobby.

Food Delivery Services

Some people decide that Meal Planning and Meal Prep is just not a realistic lifestyle for them. They may live a busier life than average, have a big active family, hate to cook, can't cook, don't want to cook, hate shopping, not creative, and more reasons. These people may choose to use a meal planning/prep or food delivery service to assist them with their meals.

Sometimes this can be costly, sometimes it may be affordable, but what it is, is convenient and by using this service you are still preparing in advance for what life throws at you during this change. You are still choosing healthier options, and being creative in what you eat.

Journaling

This lifestyle change will change your life forever. One day you will have changed so much that you may want to share your journey with others. If you decide to share, what better way to share than to go back and see how you felt each day or a few days. It is best practice tojournal while you go through this journey. Journaling can be helpful in discovering what your negative triggers are, tracking your weight and measurement progress, tracking your feelings towards food, tracking your growth toward meal planning and food shopping and eating out and chosen food options, tracking your every step along the way. Your first journal entry should note why you are doing IF and explain your goals.

Sometimes people go as far as to go back to school for nutrition, or to be a trainer, life coach, and more, this journal will only assist you in tracking it all in real time. Your journal could be the road to success for someone or some other people who feel as though you once felt. This can also help you when you have those hard days and want to give up. Journaling can only help you on this journey; it is best practice for success.

Family Lifestyle Change

I wouldn't recommend making a drastic change, but after a few days maybe a week it's a good idea to start your family and sometimes even the company you keep around you to start eating what you eat and when you eat. If you are the cook and shopper in your house, this will be a better use of your time. You will only have to meal plan once, shop once, and cook a few meals that will feed everyone for a couple of days. Hopefully, this gives you more time during the week to add in exercise if you don't, or if you do maybe a second workout, or maybe give you a few hours of time each day to do something else you have been wanting to do, like maybe writing a book.

Brush your Teeth Earlier

Everyone should brush their teeth before bed each night. With intermittent fasting, it's better to practice brushing your teeth after your last meal. The taste of toothpaste and/orListerine should keep you from wanting to do any further eating. This is just a mind trick, but it has been a successful, helpful trick that I still use.

How to Order at Restaurants

Know the menu before you go. I repeat, know the menu before you go. Most restaurants, even fast-food restaurants, have websites in which you can view their menu options. If you know what's on the menu before you go, you can be proactive in deciding what you will order as the best option for you. Have a few staple times that most restaurants offer: grilled salmon, chicken breast, shrimp, any seafood, fried chicken wings no breading or sauce, burgers wrapped in lettuce, salads, and more.

Most restaurants DO NOT serve appropriate portions of food. This is an advertising mechanism for the restaurants; it is an effective way for them to get you to continually come back and spend money with them. I mean, who wants to go to a restaurant that serves those small plate options? Most restaurants serve 2 and sometimes 3 times the portion that a person should be eating in one sitting.

To ensure you spend your money wisely but getting the food you pay for, while simultaneously ensuring that you are using good portion control, when you order at a restaurant it is good practice to go ahead and ask for a to-go plate and when your food arrives, split your food up by keeping an appropriate portion to eat now and package away the other 2 or 3 servings for later options.

Lunch Bag Prep

Every evening after dinner, clean the kitchen and prepare for the next day. This includes preparing my lunch bag for the next day. I add the following to my lunch bag each day. 2 full meals, 3-4 snacks, and 2-3 bottles of water and sparkling water. Although most days, I eat dinner at home, what if I didn't make it home in time to eat dinner, or what if football practice goes long, what if traffic is a mess due to an accident, what if

I must work late, what if, what if, what if. Always be prepared and you will be successful. I have had unplanned events, which have forced me to eat in the car, and sometimes dinner is a few healthy snacks because I didn't have my meal with me. Be prepared.

How to Deal with Unplanned Events

Although unplanned life events occur, sometimes 3-4 times a week, as an intermittent faster, you still need to have a plan for the unplanned. Always have that lunch box/bag with you as previously mentioned. Know a few staple food options that are your go-to food options when you are on the go and don't have your own available food options. Think before you eat always.

Peer pressure is real, especially at social events, be sure to have a serious conversation with family and friends so they know you are serious and that they should not offer you items when it is not your feeding window and that your new lifestyle is not a joking matter and that you would appreciate they take it as an important part of your life. Make good decisions and be proud of those decisions that you make. Every now and then, I change my feeding windows for social events. I sometimes fast longer so that I can push my feeding window back to be able to attend social events and have dinner and drinks with family and friends.

Buy in Bulk

You may be thinking how is buying in buck related to intermittent fasting. It is vital for beginners and sometimes long time intermittent fasters to always have food on hand to accommodate any cravings and their feeding windows. It is best practice to buy favorite snack foods in bulk if available. When you buy these items in bulk you can then use small ziplock and/or sandwich bags to create your own individual serving size (according to the food label) baggies to keep in your car, purse, backpack, at school, at work, in your gym bag, in your lunch box or bag, and more.

It saves you money buying in bulk than to buy individual items already prepackage, companies charge more for convenience, so when you buy prepackaged small cute individually packaged items, it costs more than buying in bulk and doing this yourself. This also ensures that you are only having a serving or 2 according to the food label. This also saves you from not being prepared and eating unplanned food items.

Consistent Routine

Appetite is trainable because it is driven by routine. Our bodies know and learn our routines, we are usually hungry when we expect to be hungry, not necessarily when we are physically hunger, again it could be that weare bored or need fluids. Practice makes perfect, right? Fasting is a skill that with intermittent fasting, you are trying to advance this skill.

Best practice would be at least start with a good routined new life as you endure this lifestyle change. That means to set your alarm and wake to start most days at the same time, specifically during the week to start. Eat your first meal and the second meal at the same times; you can have your snacks at whatever time during the feeding window. It is also best practice to workout at the same time of the day most days and take measurements, pictures, and weigh yourself on these same days. Meal plan the week before you will shop and cook the meals. Then shop on the same day, and cook and prep the meals on the same day so you start the week always with good habits.

Setbacks

Setbacks are sometimes inevitable when it comes to any type of life change; intermittent fasting is no different. Setbacks can include general fasting knowledge, lack of discipline, willpower, self-control, fear of missing out, lack of planning or procrastination, illnesses, that may or may not include medications, that prevent this type of fasting, lack of motivation, resistance to change, YOU, and much more.

YOU

You will be your biggest setback, challenge, and critic during this attempt to change. Many people have issues with confidence, self-esteem, feeling deserving, discipline, consistency, peer pressure, unawareness, and more, which ALL can contribute to YOU being your worst nightmare during this change and ultimately maybe your demise in many aspects of life.

You must realize you are the only person who can make a change in your life, and that goes for all the changes you want to make. You are responsible for your own happiness and if changing your eating lifestyle is what will make you happier, then this information gives you the knowledge to be able to make this change without help from anyone else. You can make this change happen for YOU, and only you. You should be beginning this journal to please only you and not just for appearance purposes, but for through and through happiness and well-being.

You must believe in yourself. You must know that you are your #1 priority and must be your biggest supporter. If no one else cares, you must care enough to change your habits and be consistent in the changes you decide to make. No one should be able to derail you from making such an important change in your life.

You are responsible for your choices. This is a lifestyle change, so if you mess up, just do better the next time, don't quit on yourself. Don't make decisions based on temporary needs or feelings; think about what you do as you do it to make decisions that are better for you overall in the future. Think about your future, do you want to be trying another diet in another 30 days? Do you still want to be in the same body with the same health in 30 days? Would you rather feel comfortable in your clothes and skin and feel healthy throughout?

Practice Makes Perfect

Getting acquainted with the process of fasting in general and testing your chosen time frames for your feeding and fasting windows can be a difficult time if you are used to eating many meals/snacks daily. Being motivated to continue to develop in this change is just as important as anything else that comes along with this change. Live each day separately, as in if something did not go to your liking one day, change your process the next until you have feeding and fasting windows that work well with your daily routine schedule. Mind over matter, you matter, so make sure your mind continues to know this fact to ensure you aren't resistant to this change.

Don't be Weak

During the initial change stage, there must be an increased amount of willpower, discipline, and self-control. You will be required to practice your self-control around others who are NOT on an intermittent fasting lifestyle. You need to have the willpower to refrain from ingesting calories during their fasting window. You need to have the discipline to create these time frames and stick to them, and when the feeding and/or fasting windows are broken, create consequences for yourself to ensure it does not happen again until it does not happen anymore.

Fear of Missing Out (FOMO)

Because of how you are used to living your life, sometimes you may feel like you are missing out on the fun surrounding social and/or family eating events, but consider the fact that you are making this change to perfect how you feel and how you look to ensure you are around for a long life to enjoy life. Family and friends may not be on this lifestyle and either will or will not support this change. Alcohol should be consumed in moderation. If you choose to drink alcohol, two or less daily drinks should be the max. Choose non-sugary spirits and alcohol volume dry wines to ensure you are getting the best buzz for your choice.

Holidays will more than likely be the biggest change for you and the biggest day to test you when new to this lifestyle. Holidays are all about eating and tasting everything with family and friends and making memories. Try to prepare in advance by either assisting with cooking to ensure meals are ready before/during your feeding window and choose your favorites to ensure you are satisfied and not as vulnerable after your feeding window closes. The holidays will test you.

Prepare, Don't Procrastinate

Preparation is key. Now that you have decided on your feeding window, ALWAYS, make sure you have your meals/snacks readily available during these times. Stay ahead of your schedule a day or so, to ensure you pack your meals/snacks if you are away from home when it is time to eat those meals/snacks to ensure. Even if you plan to be home, always make sure you take at least a few snack options with your wherever you go, by preparing in this way you ensure not to ever get caught out and about for hours with nothing to eat just wasting your feeding window away.

Not Reading Labels and Controlling Portions

Although your calories are NOT restricted when intermittent fasting, eating too much of even healthy foods can lead to weight gain no matter the type of diet/lifestyle you are following. To prevent this type of setback meal plan, use portion control, be consistent with choosing the most nutritious food choices, and measure your foods to ensure you are not eating too many servings in one meal.

Nonsense from Others

There are times in life when it's better to keep your goals to yourself. Keep your goals away from negative people, specifically keep negative people away from your goals and out of your life. To be successful in many things in life, you need a support system, which does not include negative people. You need someone who can cheer you on, someone who can motivate you, someone, who may be willing to join you, someone who doesn't add to your problems by persuading you to do what is against your goals. If you have these types of people in your life, do not tell them your plan of intermittent fasting.

Many people have their own preconceived assumptions about fasting, and intermittent fasting, and usually their views are without researched knowledge and education. It is important that you understand and know myth versus facts when it comes to intermittent fasting. People who have tried all types of diets seem to think they know them all, and they are very discouraging at times. During a lifestyle change as intermittent fasting, it is very easy to get discouraged, so stay the course and keep those people away, while you try this out yourself based on your researched facts.

Chapter 8:
Recipes

Breakfast recipes
Choco Chip Whey Waffles

Serves:2

Prep time: 10 minutes

Cooking Time: 6 minutes

Ingredients:

- 2-tbsp organic coconut oil
- 2-tbsp coconut sugar
- 4-tbsp chocolate whey protein powder
- ⅓-cup almond flour
- A pinch of salt
- ½-tsp baking powder
- ½-cup almond milk
- 2-pcs eggs

Directions:

1. Mix all the ingredients in the blender to obtain a homogenous paste.

2. Preheat your waffle iron. Pour the waffle dough in the iron and cook each waffle for 3 minutes.

Nutritional Values per Serving:

Calories: 423

Fat: 32.8g

Protein: 26.5g

Total Carbohydrates: 8.3g

Dietary Fiber: 2.9g

Net Carbohydrates: 5.4g

Coco Cinnamon-Packed Pancakes

Serves:2

Prep time: 30 minutes

Cooking Time: 5 minutes

Ingredients:

- 2-pcs eggs

- 2½-tbsp organic coconut flour

- ¼-cup milk substitute with hydrogenated vegetable oil (or almond milk)

- 1-tbsp baking soda

- ½-tbsp cinnamon

- ½-tbsp baobab powder

- 2-tbsp organic coconut flower syrup

Directions:

1. In a salad bowl, mix the coconut flour, baobab powder, cinnamon, and baking soda.

2. Add the beaten eggs, the almond milk, and the coconut syrup. Let the dough rest for 30 minutes.

3. Cook the pancakes in a hot pan with coconut oil.

4. Dress the pancakes with raspberries/blueberries or almonds.

Nutritional Values per Serving:

Calories: 392

Fat: 32.5g

Protein: 20g

Total Carbohydrates: 11.3g

Dietary Fiber: 6.4g

Net Carbohydrates: 4.9g

Magdalena Muffins with Tart Tomatoes

Serves:2

Prep time: 10 minutes

Cooking Time: 20 minutes

Ingredients:

- 2½-tbsp whole-wheat flour
- 2½-tbsp almond flour
- 1-tbsp yeast or baking soda
- A dash of salt, pepper, and paprika
- 2-pcs eggs
- 1-tbsp organic cashew nuts
- 1-tbsp hemp oil
- 2½-tbsp soymilk
- ⅓-cup feta cheese, diced
- 1⅓-cup dried tomatoes, without oil and sliced into small pieces

Directions:

1. Mix the wheat flour, almond flour, yeast, and spices.

2. Then add eggs, cashews, oil, and soymilk.

3. Mix well to obtain a smooth paste. Add the feta and tomatoes.

4. Mix well and pour the dough into muffin pans previously greased with coconut oil.

5. Bake for 20 minutes at 350°F.

Nutritional Values per Serving:

Calories: 405

Fat: 33.3g

Protein: 20.3g

Total Carbohydrates: 11g

Dietary Fiber: 4.9g

Net Carbohydrates: 6.1g

Spinach Shoots Mediterranean Medley

Serves: 2

Prep time: 10 minutes

Cooking Time: 1 minute

Ingredients:

- ½-cup spinach shoots
- 2-tbsp quinoa
- ¼-cup avocado, sliced
- 1-tbsp fresh goat cheese
- 1-tsp agave syrup, gluten-free
- ¼-cup dried blackberries

- 1-pc fig
- 1-tsp pumpkin seeds puree

Directions:

1. Arrange the spinach shoots, cooked quinoa, and avocado on a large plate.

2. Mix the goat cheese, agave syrup, and dried blackberries.

3. Make 4 small cuts in the fig so that you can open it and insert the goat cheese mixture.

4. Spread your fig on the spinach shoots. Sprinkle over with pumpkin seed puree.

Nutritional Values per Serving:

Calories: 308

Fat: 26g

Protein: 15.4g

Total Carbohydrates: 9.7g

Dietary Fiber: 6.5g

Net Carbohydrates: 3.2g

Romantic Raspberry Power Pancake

Serves:1

Prep time: 5 minutes

Cooking Time: 10 minutes

Ingredients:

- 2-tbsp raspberries, crushed
- 2-tsp almond flour
- 1-tbsp yeast or baking soda
- 1-tbsp vegan protein powder
- 2-tbsp soymilk
- 1-tbsp coconut oil

Directions:

1. Mix the crushed raspberries and dry ingredients.
2. Pour the milk and mix well to obtain a homogenous mixture.
3. Cook the pancakes for 2 minutes on each side using a little coconut oil in a pan. Flip the pancake when small bubbles appear.
4. Dress with almonds or nuts.

Nutritional Values per Serving:

Calories: 323

Fat: 25.3g

Protein: 15.7g

Total Carbohydrates: 12g

Dietary Fiber: 3.8g

Net Carbohydrates: 4.8g

Spinach Sausage Feta Frittata

Serves: 6

Prep Time: 15 minutes

Cooking Time: 30 minutes

Ingredients:

- 10-oz. spinach, frozen, thawed, drained, and chopped
- 12-oz. sausage, sliced into small pieces
- ½-cup feta cheese, crumbled
- ½-cup almond milk, unsweetened
- ½-cup heavy cream
- ¼-tsp. ground nutmeg
- ½-tsp. salt
- ¼-tsp. black pepper
- 12-pcs eggs, whisked

Directions:

1. Place the sausage in a medium-sized mixing bowl. Break the spinach up into the same bowl as the sausage.

2. Sprinkle the cheese over the mixture. Toss lightly until fully combined. Lightly spread the mixture onto a greased 13" × 9" casserole dish, or greased muffin cups.

3. In a larger bowl, blend the almond milk, cream, nutmeg, salt, and pepper with the eggs, and mix well until fully combined.

4. Gently pour the mixture into the dish or muffin cups until for about ¾ full. Bake at 375°F for about 50 minutes (for the casserole), or 30 minutes (for the muffin cups), or until fully set.

Nutritional Values per Serving:

Calories: 295

Fat: 22.9g

Protein: 18.5g

Total Carbohydrates: 4.6g

Dietary Fiber: 1g

Net Carbohydrates: 3.6g

Mayonnaise Mixed with Energy Egg

Serves: 1

Prep Time: 2 minutes

Cooking Time: 5 minutes

Ingredients:

- 2-tbsp organic mayonnaise, gluten-free
- 1-pc large egg
- 1-tbsp butter

Directions:

1. Mix the mayonnaise and egg in a medium-sized bowl until fully combined.

2. Melt the butter in a non-stick skillet. Pour the egg mixture, and cook until set. Scrape the egg and all remaining fat onto a serving plate. Serve immediately.

Nutritional Values per Serving:

Calories: 295

Fat: 22.7g

Protein: 18.8g

Total Carbohydrates: 3.8g

Dietary Fiber: 0.1g

Net Carbohydrates: 3.7g

Avocados atop Toasted Tartiné

Serves: 2

Prep Time: 10 minutes

Cooking Time: 5 minutes

Ingredients:

- 2-slices bread, gluten-free
- ½-pc small avocado, thinly sliced
- 1-tbsp fresh cheese
- 1-tsp lemon juice
- A dash of salt and pepper
- 1-tsp chia seeds for garnish (optional)

Directions:

1. Toast lightly the bread slices.
2. Carefully arrange the avocado slices on each bread slice. Drizzle with the lemon juice. Spread the fresh cheese. Sprinkle with pepper and salt. Top with garnish.

Nutritional Values per Serving:

Calories: 268

Fat: 22.4g

Protein: 13.5g

Total Carbohydrates: 8.9g

Dietary Fiber: 6.7g

Net Carbohydrates: 3.2g

Fish Fillet & Perky Potato Cheese Combo

Serves: 2

Prep Time: 15 minutes

Cooking Time: 10 minutes

Ingredients:

- 1-tbsp olive oil
- 1-pc large potato, cooked and thinly sliced
- ¼-cup lean white cheese
- ½-tsp herbs of your choice
- 3.5-oz. herring fillet, steamed and sliced in half
- ½-tsp flaxseed oil or coconut oil
- A dash of salt and pepper

Directions:

1. Heat a non-stick pan with olive oil. Add potato slices and cook for several minutes until browned.

2. Season the white cheese with salt, pepper, and herbs of your choice.

3. Arrange the potatoes equally between two plates. Top with the cheese and herring fillets. Garnish with a drizzle of flaxseed oil.

Nutritional Values per Serving:

Calories: 298

Fat: 24.9g

Protein: 14.2g

Total Carbohydrates: 6.5g

Dietary Fiber: 3.2g

Net Carbohydrates: 4.3g

Cream Cheese Protein Pancake

Serves: 2

Prep Time: 10 minutes

Cooking Time: 12 minutes

Ingredients:

- 2-pcs eggs
- 2-oz cream cheese
- 1-packet sweetener
- ½-tsp cinnamon
- 1-tbsp butter

Directions:

1. Mix all the ingredients in a blender except the butter. Blend until smooth. Let the batter stand for 2 minutes to allow the bubbles to settle.

2. Grease slightly a hot pan with ¼-tbsp butter. Pour ¼-batter into the pan. Cook for about 2 minutes until turning golden. Flip the pancake and cook for 1 minute on its other side.

3. Repeat the same cooking procedure with the remaining batter. Serve with fresh berries of choice and sugar-free syrup.

Nutritional Values per Serving:

Calories: 340

Fat: 28.1g

Protein: 16.2g

Total Carbohydrates: 8.1g

Dietary Fiber: 3.8g

Net Carbohydrates: 4.3g

Veggie Variety with Peanut Paste

Serves: 1

Prep Time: 15 minutes

Cooking Time: 15 minutes

Ingredients:

- 1-bulb small onion, thinly sliced
- ¾-cup broccoli, sliced into quarters
- 1-pc small carrot, sliced into quarters
- ½-pc green pepper, thinly sliced
- 5-pcs mushrooms, sliced into quarters
- A dash of salt, pepper, and powdered chili
- 2-tbsp peanut butter, dairy-free

- 2-tbsp. soy sauce, gluten-free

- 1-tbsp agave syrup (or honey), gluten-free

- ¼-cup red cabbage, thinly sliced

Directions:

1. Pour a little water in a heated skillet and cook the onions until they are transparent. Add the broccoli, carrot, pepper, and mushrooms. Cook for 10 minutes until tender. (Add some water if the pan is too dry). Season the veggies with a dash of salt, pepper, and chili.

2. For the sauce, mix the peanut butter with the soy sauce, agave syrup, and 3 tbsp water.

3. To serve, incorporate the red cabbage. Garnish the dish with the sauce.

Nutritional Values per Serving:

Calories: 349

Fat: 28.7g

Protein: 18.4g

Total Carbohydrates: 10.8g

Dietary Fiber: 6.5g

Net Carbohydrates: 4.3g

Avocado Aliment with Egg Element

Serves: 2

Prep Time: 8 minutes

Cooking Time: 20 minutes

Ingredients:

- 1 egg, whisked
- 1 avocado, halved, pitted, and removed slightly with flesh
- A dash of sea salt and pepper
- 1-tbsp parsley, chopped
- 1-tsp cayenne pepper

Directions:

1. Preheat your oven to 375°F.

2. Pour the egg gently into each halved avocado. Remove the excess liquid.

3. Place the stuffed avocado in a baking tray. Bake for 20 minutes.

4. Season the preparation with sea salt, parsley, and cayenne pepper.

Nutritional Values per Serving:

Calories: 275

Fat: 23.8g

Protein: 11.8g

Total Carbohydrates: 10.7g

Dietary Fiber: 4g

Net Carbohydrates: 3.4g

Pumpkin Pancakes

Serves: 3

Prep Time: 10 minutes

Cooking Time: 30 minutes

Ingredients:

- 1-tsp vanilla extract
- 1-cup coconut cream
- 3-pcs eggs
- 2-tbsp egg whites
- ½-cup pumpkin puree
- 5-packs sweetener
- 4-tbsp ground flax seed
- 4-tbsp ground hazelnuts or hazelnut flour
- 1-tsp yeast or baking powder
- 1-tbsp black tea powder
- 1-tbsp. coconut oil for cooking

Directions:

1. Whisk together the first five liquid ingredients for half a minute until they become frothy. Mix the dry ingredients in a separate bowl.

2. Combine both the dry and liquid ingredients to obtain a batter. (Add water, as necessary if the mixture is too thick.)

3. Grease a saucepan with a teaspoon of coconut oil. Ladle in the first pancake.

4. Cover the pan and cook for 3 minutes. Flip and cook the other side.

5. Repeat the cooking process until using up all the batter.

Nutritional Values per Serving:

Calories: 200

Fat: 16.4g

Protein: 11g

Total Carbohydrates: 5.2g

Dietary Fiber: 3g

Net Carbohydrates: 2.2g

Whole-Wheat Plain Pancakes

Serves: 1

Prep Time: 5 minutes

Cooking Time: 12 minutes

Ingredients:

- 2-pcs eggs
- 4-tbsp whole-wheat flour
- ½-tsp yeast or baking soda
- ⅓-cup sunflower oil
- 1-tbsp coconut oil for cooking

Directions:

1. Mix all the ingredients in a bowl until obtaining a smooth consistency.

2. Pour the coconut oil in a pan placed over medium heat. Cook for 3 minutes until browned. Flip and cook the other side.

3. Serve hot and garnish with fresh fruits of your choice such as blueberries, strawberries or raspberries, nuts, and coconut flakes.

Nutritional Values per Serving:

Calories: 329

Fat: 27.6g

Protein: 16.1g

Total Carbohydrates: 5.4g

Dietary Fiber: 1.3g

Net Carbohydrates: 4.4g

Blueberries Breakfast Bowl

Serves: 1

Prep Time: 35 minutes

Cooking Time: 0 minutes

Ingredients:

- 1-tsp chia seeds
- 1-cup almond milk
- ¼-cup fresh blueberries or fresh fruits
- 1-pack sweetener for taste

Directions:

1. Mix the chia seeds with almond milk. Stir periodically.
2. Place in the fridge to cool for 30 minutes, and then serve with fresh fruit. Enjoy!

Nutritional Values per Serving:

Calories: 202

Fat: 16.8g

Protein: 10.2g

Total Carbohydrates: 9.8g

Dietary Fiber: 5.8g

Net Carbohydrates: 2.6g

Feta-Filled Tomato-Topped Oldie Omelet

Serves: 1

Prep Time: 5 minutes

Cooking Time: 6 minutes

Ingredients:

- 1-tbsp coconut oil
- 2-pcs eggs
- 1½-tbsp milk
- A dash of salt and pepper
- ¼-cup tomatoes, sliced into cubes
- 2-tbsp feta cheese, crumbled

Directions:

1. Beat the eggs with the pepper, salt, milk, and the remaining spices.

2. Pour the mixture into a heated pan with coconut oil.

3. Stir in the tomatoes and cheese. Cook for 6 minutes or until the cheese melts.

Nutritional Values per Serving:

Calories: 335

Fat: 28.4g

Protein: 16.2g

Total Carbohydrates: 4.5g

Dietary Fiber: 0.8g

Net Carbohydrates: 3.7g

Ave Avocado Super Smoothie

Serves: 1

Prep Time: 10 minutes

Cooking Time: 1 minute

Ingredients:

- ½-cup Greek yogurt
- 7-oz. frozen avocados
- ½-cup water
- ½-tsp vanilla powder
- 1-tsp each chia seeds, chocolate chips, and peanut butter for garnish

Directions:

1. Mix all the ingredients. You can also use a blender to crush them.

2. Pour the smoothie into a bowl and garnish to your taste with fruits, seeds or nuts.

Nutritional Values per Serving:

Calories: 398

Fat: 33.1g

Protein: 20g

Total Carbohydrates: 15.5g

Dietary Fiber: 10.6g

Net Carbohydrates: 4.9g

Hearty Hodgepodge

Serves: 1

Prep Time: 5 minutes

Cooking Time: 25 minutes

Ingredients:

- 1-bulb small onion, diced

- 1-tbsp coconut oil

- 1-tbsp bacon bits

- 1-pc medium zucchini, diced into squares

- 1-tbsp parsley or chives, chopped

- ¼-tsp. of salt

- 1-pc large egg, fried

Directions:

1. Sauté the onion with coconut oil in a pan placed over medium heat. Add the bacon, stirring frequently until both onion and bacon turn slightly brown.

2. Add the zucchini, and cook for 15 minutes. Remove from heat and transfer the preparation in a serving bowl. Sprinkle over the parsley.

3. To serve, top the dish with the fried egg.

Nutritional Values per Serving:

Calories: 290

Fat: 24g

Protein: 14.6g

Total Carbohydrates: 6.7g

Dietary Fiber: 3.1g

Net Carbohydrates: 3.6g

Chocolate Chia Plain Pudding

Serves: 3

Prep Time: 55 minutes

Cooking Time: 0 minutes

Ingredients:

*   3-tbsp chia seeds

*   2-cups water

- ¼-cup whey chocolate protein

- ½-cup Greek yogurt, sugar-free

- ¼-cup linseeds, roasted

- 1-tbsp cocoa powder, unsweetened

- 1-packet sweetener (optional)

Directions:

1. Add chia seeds to a bowl of water and let stand for 20 minutes while occasionally stirring.

2. When chia seeds are inflated, add the other ingredients and mix again.

3. Refrigerate for 30 minutes before serving.

Nutritional Values per Serving:

Calories: 370

Fat: 28.7g

Protein: 22.3g

Total Carbohydrates: 10.8g

Dietary Fiber: 5.2g

Net Carbohydrates: 5.6g

Seasoned Sardines with Sunny Side

Serves: 1

Prep Time: 5 minutes

Cooking Time: 10 minutes

Ingredients:

- 2-oz. sardines in olive oil

- 2-pcs eggs

- ½-cup arugula

- ¼-cup artichoke hearts, diced

- A pinch of salt

- A dash of black pepper

Directions:

1. Preheat your oven to 375°F.

2. Place the sardines in an oven-ready stoneware bowl. Add the eggs on top of the sardines. Top the eggs with the arugula and artichokes. Sprinkle with salt and pepper.

3. Bake for 10 minutes until the eggs cook through.

Nutritional Values per Serving:

Calories: 255

Fat: 21g

Protein: 13.5g

Total Carbohydrates: 4.9g

Dietary Fiber: 1.8g

Net Carbohydrates: 3.1g

Healthy Breakfast Burritos

Serves: 4

Prep time - 5 mins

Cooking time - 10 mins

Ingredients

- 8 eggs
- 1 tbsp milk
- 1 tbsp garlic, minced
- 1 red pepper, minced
- Half an onion, red if possible, minced
- 4 slices of bacon, cooked
- Salt
- Pepper
- 4 tortilla wraps (multi-grain or wholegrain)
- little cheese (optional)

Directions:

1. Take a medium-sized saucepan and heat over a medium heat

2. Add the garlic and cook for a couple of minutes, until fragrant

3. Whisk the eggs with the milk and place to one side

4. Add the pepper and onion to the pan and allow to cook for a couple more minutes

5. Add the eggs to the pan and cook for 4 minutes

6. Once cooked, add a quarter of the egg mixture onto each tortilla wrap and add one piece of the bacon on top

7. You can add cheese if you want, although it isn't necessary

8. Wrap up and enjoy it!

Nutritional Values per Serving:

Calories: 352

Carbs: 22g

Fat: 20g

Protein: 8g

Lunch recipes

Pulled Pepper-Lemon Loins

Serves: 4-servings

Prep time: 15 minutes

Cooking Time: 240-360 minutes

Ingredients

- ½-stick of butter
- 1-pc large lemon, sliced
- 1-pc green pepper, chopped
- 1-tbsp garlic, minced
- 2-tbsp olive oil
- 1-tbsp salt

- 1-tsp dried thyme

- ½-tbsp Dijon mustard

- 3-lbs. (4-pcs) chicken tenderloins

- 1-cheddar cheese slice, shredded

- 4-leaves romaine lettuce

Directions:

1. Combine the butter, lemon, pepper, garlic, oil, salt, thyme, and mustard in your slow cooker. Switch the slow cooker on high and melt the butter.

2. Add the chicken; ensure to coat the chicken with the butter mixture.

3. Cook on high for 4 hours or on low for 6 hours. Add the cheese and let it sit for 15 minutes on low.

4. To serve, place the chicken over a bed of lettuce leaves.

Nutritional Values per Serving:

Calories: 280

Fat: 23.3g

Protein: 14g

Total Carbohydrates: 4.1g

Dietary Fiber: 0.6g

Net Carbohydrates: 3.5g

Shrimps & Spinach Spaghetti

Serves: 2

Prep time: 5 minutes

Cooking Time: 8 minutes

Ingredients:

- 8-tbsp vegetable broth
- 1-cup low carb spaghetti, rinsed and drained
- 1-pc leek, cut into strips
- 1⅓-cup frozen peas
- 1⅓-cup fresh spinach leaves
- ¼-lb. shrimp, pre-cooked
- 1-tbsp lemon zest

- 1-pc green pepper, finely chopped (divided, per serving)

- 2-pcs basil leaves (divided, per serving)

- 1-pc lemon (divided, per serving)

Directions:

1. Pour the vegetable broth in a wok and cook for 5 minutes. Add the leeks, peas, spinach, and shrimp. Cook further for 5 minutes.

2. Add the spaghetti, and continue cooking for 2 minutes. Remove quickly from heat and pour into a bowl, mix with lemon zest.

3. Divide the pasta equally between two plates. To serve, garnish with the pepper, basil leaves, and lemon.

Nutritional Values per Serving:

Calories: 425

Fat: 33g

Protein: 25g

Total Carbohydrates: 15.7g

Dietary Fiber: 10.4g

Net Carbohydrates: 5.3g

Single Skillet Seafood-Filled Frittata

Serves:4

Prep time: 2 minutes

Cooking Time: 18 minutes

Ingredients:

- 1-pc green pepper
- ¼-pc lime, squeezed for juice
- 1-tbsp coconut flour
- 1-tbsp sesame oil
- 1-tbsp soy sauce, gluten-free
- 1-tbsp coconut oil
- 3-bulbs fresh onions, chopped
- ½-clove garlic, minced
- ¼-cup prawns, raw
- 1⅓-cup mussels, deshelled
- 2-pcs eggs, whisked

Directions:

1. Preheat your oven to 475°F. Meanwhile, make the sauce by combining the first five ingredients in a mixing bowl. Mix thoroughly until fully combined. Set aside.

2. Melt the coconut oil in a small skillet and fry the onions. Add the garlic, prawns, and mussels. Cook for 10 minutes until the prawns turn pink.

3. Stir in the eggs. Place the skillet in the oven and bake for 5 minutes.

4. Slice the frittata in four slices and serve with the sauce.

Nutritional Values per Serving:

Calories: 459

Fat: 38.2g

Protein: 22.9g

Total Carbohydrates: 8.7g

Dietary Fiber: 3g

Net Carbohydrates: 5.7g

Poultry Pâté & Creamy Crackers

Serves:1

Prep time: 15 minutes

Cooking Time: 35 minutes

Ingredients:

- 3.5-oz. chicken livers
- 3-tbsp butter, softened
- 1-tsp. Italian seasoning

- A pinch of salt and pepper
- 3-pcs unsalted creamy crackers, gluten-free

Directions:

1. Put all the ingredients in a blender apart from the crackers. Blend to a smooth paste consistency.

2. Serve with the crackers.

Nutritional Values per Serving:

Calories: 437

Fat: 36.4g

Protein: 21.9g

Total Carbohydrates: 5.5g

Dietary Fiber: 0g

Net Carbohydrates: 5.5g

Chickpeas Carrots Curry

Serves:1

Prep time: 5 minutes

Cooking Time: 25 minutes

Ingredients:

- ½-bulb onion, finely chopped
- ½-pc carrot, sliced into cubes
- ½-tsp coconut oil

- ¼-cup chickpeas

- ½-tsp tomato paste

- 3-tbsp light soy cream

- ½-tsp turmeric powder

- ⅛-bunch fresh coriander

- A pinch of salt, pepper, and sweet paprika

Directions:

1. Sauté the onions and carrots for 5 minutes with coconut oil in a skillet.

2. Add the chickpeas, tomato paste, soy cream, turmeric, coriander, and spices. Mix well and cook for 10 minutes.

3. Cook the rice for 10 minutes in boiling water. Serve the konjac rice with the vegetable curry and chickpeas.

Nutritional Values per Serving:

Calories: 380

Fat: 30.9g

Protein: 18g

Total Carbohydrates: 14.4g

Dietary Fiber: 10.7g

Net Carbohydrates: 3.7g

Baked Broccoli in Olive Oil

Serves: 3

Prep Time: 5 minutes

Cooking Time: 25 minutes

Ingredients:

- 1½-lbs broccoli florets
- ¼-cup olive oil
- 3-tsps. garlic, minced
- 2-tbsp fresh basil, chopped
- ½-tsp red chili flakes
- ¾-tsp kosher salt
- Zest of ½-pc lemon
- Juice of ½-pc lemon
- ⅓-cup parmesan cheese

Directions:

1. Preheat your oven to 425°F.

2. Arrange the broccoli florets in a baking sheet lined with parchment paper.

3. Season the broccoli with olive oil, chopped fresh basil, minced garlic, kosher salt, red chili flakes, zest and juice of half a lemon each.

4. Sprinkle parmesan cheese over the broccoli. Place the sheet in the oven to bake for about 25 minutes.

Nutritional Values per Serving:

Calories: 484

Fat: 39.2g

Protein: 26.7g

Total Carbohydrates: 21.6g

Dietary Fiber: 16.8g

Net Carbohydrates: 4.8g

Bunless Bacon Burger

Serves: 4

Prep Time: 8 minutes

Cooking Time: 37 minutes

Ingredients:

- 1½-lbs. ground beef
- 2-tbsp olive oil
- 2-tbsp bacon bits
- 4-oz. pepper jack cheese
- 1-bulb onion, sliced crosswise
- 8-leaves romaine lettuce
- A dash of salt and pepper

Directions:

1. Form the ground beef into four patties. Cook for 4 minutes with olive oil on a skillet placed over medium heat. Flip the patties to cook the other sides. Set aside.

2. Using the same skillet, stir-fry the bacon bits for 5 minutes until crispy.

3. Use the lettuce leaves as buns. Place each patty on a leaf and top with the bacon bits. Sprinkle a dash of salt and pepper. Top each burger with the cheese to melt.

Nutritional Values per Serving:

Calories: 435

Fat: 36.3g

Protein: 21.7g

Total Carbohydrates: 6.1g

Dietary Fiber: 0.7g

Net Carbohydrates: 5.4g

Smoky Sage Sausage

Serves: 4

Prep Time: 5 minutes

Cooking Time: 8 minutes

Ingredients:

- 2-tbsp sage, chopped
- 2-packets sweetener
- 1-tsp salt
- 1-tsp maple extract
- 1-lb. ground pork
- ½-tsp black pepper
- ¼-tsp garlic powder
- ⅛-tsp cayenne pepper

Directions:

1. Mix all the ingredients in a mixing bowl.

2. Form patties from the mixture.

3. Put the patties in a skillet placed over medium heat. Cook for 4 minutes until cooked through. Flip the patties to cook on the other side.

Nutritional Values per Serving:

Calories: 170

Fat: 13.2g

Protein: 8.4g

Total Carbohydrates: 5.3g

Dietary Fiber: 1g

Net Carbohydrates: 4.3g

Steamed Salmon & Salad Bento Box

Serves: 2

Prep Time: 10 minutes

Cooking Time: 0 minutes

Ingredients:

- 2-pcs salad heads
- 1-cup carrot, grated
- ¼-cup cucumber, sliced
- 1-pc green pepper, thinly sliced
- 4-cups marinara pasta, rinsed, drained, and cooked for 2 minutes in boiling water
- ½-lb. salmon, steamed
- 2-pcs lemons
- 2-pcs eggs, boiled and sliced
- 1-tsp chia seeds
- 4-tbsp yogurt, sugar-free
- 1-tsp turmeric powder
- ½-pc lemon, zest
- 2-tbsp mint, minced
- A pinch of pepper

Directions:

1. Divide equally the first eight ingredients between two bento boxes. Sprinkle the arrangements with chia seeds.

2. Mix the rest of the ingredients to make the sauce. Pack the sauce separately.

Nutritional Values per Serving:

Calories: 391

Fat: 30.4g

Protein: 24.9g

Total Carbohydrates: 11.8g

Dietary Fiber: 7.3g

Net Carbohydrates: 4.5g

Stuffed Spaghetti Squash

Serves: 2

Prep Time: 30 minutes

Cooking Time: 30 minutes

Ingredients:

- 1-pc spaghetti squash, halved and pitted
- 1-tsp olive oil
- ½-cup bacon strips, grilled
- 3-cups ground beef

- 1-pc green pepper, thinly sliced
- ½-bulb onion, sliced into cubes
- 1-tsp garlic powder
- 1-tsp paprika
- A pinch of salt and pepper
- 1-cup cheddar cheese, grated

Directions:

1. Rub the squash halves with oil, and bake for 30 minutes at 350°F.

2. Meanwhile, roast the bacon in a saucepan placed over high heat. Stir in the onion and pepper. Add the beef and spices. Use salt and pepper to season the mixture and cook for 15 minutes, stirring regularly. Set aside.

3. Remove the flesh of the cooked squash by scratching with a fork. Mix the flesh with the meat mixture. Add the cheese, and put the mixture in the frayed squash.

4. Return the stuffed squash to the hot oven, and bake for 10 minutes.

Nutritional Values per Serving:

Calories: 404

Fat: 33.2g

Protein: 20.3g

Total Carbohydrates: 7g

Dietary Fiber: 1g

Net Carbohydrates: 6g

Prawn Pasta

Serves: 3

Prep Time: 10 minutes

Cooking Time: 12 minutes

Ingredients:

- 1-tsp sesame seeds
- 1-pc lime
- ½-pc green pepper, thinly sliced
- 2 tbsp coconut flour
- 2-tbsp sesame oil
- 1-tbsp soy sauce, gluten-free
- 2-heads small cabbages
- 6-bulbs small onions, chopped
- 1-cup prawns, steamed
- 3-cups low-carb pasta, rinsed, drained, and cooked for 2 minutes in boiling water
- 8-pcs small radishes, sliced into 4-pieces for garnish
- ½-pc avocado, sliced for garnish

Directions:

1. Mix the first six ingredients in a bowl to make the pasta sauce. Set aside.

2. Cook the cabbage for 10 minutes in a pan with a little water and soy sauce. Add the onions and prawns. Cook for 2 minutes.

3. Arrange the pasta in a plate, topped with the prawn mixture, pasta sauce, and the garnishing.

Nutritional Values per Serving:

Calories: 393

Fat: 32.8g

Protein: 19.7g

Total Carbohydrates: 14.9g

Dietary Fiber: 10.1g

Net Carbohydrates: 4.8g

Tasty Tofu Carrots &Cauliflower Cereal

Serves: 1

Prep Time: 20 minutes

Cooking Time: 20 minutes

Ingredients:

For the Tofu-Carrots Mix:

- ½-block extra firm tofu, crumbled

- 2-tbsp reduced sodium soy sauce, gluten-free

- ½-cup onion, diced

- 1-cup carrot, diced

- 1-tsp turmeric

For the Cauliflower Cereal:

- 3-cups riced cauliflower

- 2-tbsp reduced sodium soy sauce, gluten-free

- 1½-tsp toasted sesame oil

- 1-tbsp rice vinegar

- 1-tbsp ginger, minced

- ½-cup broccoli, finely chopped

- 2-cloves garlic, minced

- ½-cup frozen peas

Directions:

1. Toss the tofu with the rest of the tofu-carrots mix ingredients. Place the mixture in your air fryer basket. Lock the lid and cook for 10 minutes at 370°F.

2. Meanwhile, toss together all of the cauliflower cereal ingredients. Add this mixture to the air fryer pan. Lock the lid and cook for another 10 minutes at 375°F.

Nutritional Values per Serving:

Calories: 390

Fat: 32.6g

Protein: 19.5g

Total Carbohydrates: 17.4g

Dietary Fiber: 12.7g

Net Carbohydrates: 4.7g

Stuffed Straw Mushroom Mobcap

Serves: 1

Prep Time: 15 minutes

Cooking Time: 5 minutes

Ingredients:

- 1-cup fresh spinach, washed, bathed in ice, and drained
- 1-cup straw mushrooms or Chinese mushroom, washed and stems removed
- 1-tbsp coconut oil
- 1-bulb onion, finely chopped
- 1-clove garlic, minced
- A dash of salt and pepper
- A pinch of nutmeg
- ¼-cup quinoa, cooked

- 3.5-oz. cottage cheese

Directions:

1. Spread the spinach leaves over the food film while rolling them.

2. Fry the mushrooms with coconut oil in a saucepan before adding onion and garlic. Season with pepper, salt and nutmeg. Set aside.

3. Combine the cooked quinoa with the cottage cheese. Spread the mixture evenly on the spinach leaves then roll into a pudding with the help of the food film.

4. Stuff the mushroom heads with the spinach pudding, and place them in the fridge.

5. Just before serving, slice the mushroom head with a sharp knife and pass quickly to the pan to heat.

Nutritional Values per Serving:

Calories: 401

Fat: 34.7g

Protein: 17.2g

Total Carbohydrates: 16.9g

Dietary Fiber: 11.4g

Net Carbohydrates: 5g

Crispy Chicken Packed in Pandan

Serves: 4

Prep Time: 30 minutes

Cooking Time: 18 minutes

Ingredients:

- 4-pcs (½-lb.) chicken thigh
- 1-tbsp shallot
- 1-pc lemon
- 1-tsp of fennel seeds
- 1-tsp of turmeric powder
- 1-tsp of chili powder
- 1-tbsp of oyster sauce, gluten-free
- A pinch of salt
- A pinch of sugar
- A handful of pandan leaves

Directions:

1. Preheat your air fryer to 350°F for about 5 minutes.

2. Marinate the chicken with all the ingredients. Set aside for 30 minutes.

3. Wrap each chicken meat with the pandan leaves.

4. Arrange the wrapped chicken in the air fryer basket and lock the lid

5. Set to cook for 18 minutes at 375°F.

Nutritional Values per Serving:

Calories: 382

Fat: 32.5g

Protein: 17.8g

Total Carbohydrates: 7.7g

Dietary Fiber: 3.1g

Net Carbohydrates: 4.6g

Chicken Curry Masala Mix

Serves: 3

Prep Time: 10 minutes

Cooking Time: 35 minutes

Ingredients:

- 2-tbsp sesame oil (divided)

- 2-tbsp ginger, diced

- 1½-lbs chicken thighs, boneless, skinless, and diced

- 1-cup tomatoes, chopped

- ¼-cup coriander, chopped

- 2-tsp turmeric

- 1-tsp cumin
- 1-tsp cayenne
- 2-tbsp lemon juice
- Cilantro or mint leaves for garnish

Directions;

1. Sauté the ginger and jalapeno pepper with half of the sesame oil in a saucepan. Add the. Stir in the chicken, tomatoes, and coriander. Add the spices, the remaining sesame oil, lemon juice and half a cup of water.

2. Cover and cook for 30 minutes.

3. To serve, pour everything in a deep salad bowl, and garnish with cilantro or mint leaves.

Nutritional Values per Serving:

Calories: 377

Fat: 29.3g

Protein: 23.4g

Total Carbohydrates: 6.8g

Dietary Fiber: 1.9g

Net Carbohydrates: 4.9g

Milano Meatballs with Tangy Tomato

Serves: 3

Prep Time: 25 minutes

Cooking Time: 30 minutes

Ingredients:

For the Meatballs:

- 1-lb extra-lean ground beef

- 1-pc egg, whisked

- 10-pcs sun-dried tomatoes, chopped

- ½-cup ricotta cheese

- 1-cup Parmigiano-Reggiano cheese or parmesan cheese, freshly grated

- salt and freshly ground black pepper

For the Tomato Sauce:

- 1-bulb onion, finely chopped

- ¼-cup extra-virgin olive oil

- 2-lbs. tomato puree, gluten-free

- A pinch of salt and freshly ground black pepper

Directions:

1. Combine all the meatball ingredients in a mixing bowl. Mix well until fully combined. Form balls from the mixture, and pat them down for even cooking.

2. Sauté the onions with olive oil in a skillet until they are translucent. Add the tomato puree and bring to a boil. Add the remaining ingredients and the meatballs. Cook for 30 minutes on medium heat.

Nutritional Values per Serving:

Calories: 396

Fat: 32.6g

Protein: 20.9g

Total Carbohydrates: 8.2g

Dietary Fiber: 3.4g

Net Carbohydrates: 4.8g

Aubergine À la Lasagna Lunch

Serves: 2

Prep Time: 20 minutes

Cooking Time: 30 minutes

Ingredients:

- 2-pcs large eggplants, sliced and drained from excess liquid with a paper towel

- A pinch of sea salt

- 2-cups part-skim ricotta cheese

- ½-cup parmesan cheese, freshly grated

- 1-pc egg, whisked

- 4-cups homemade tomato sauce, sugar-free

- 2-tbsp part-skim mozzarella cheese, shredded

- 2-tbsp cheddar cheese, grated

- 2-tbsp parsley, chopped

Directions:

1. Preheat your oven to 375°F. Meanwhile, season the eggplant slices with salt. Grill the eggplant slices for 3 minutes on each side.

2. Combine the ricotta, parmesan, and egg in a large bowl. Set aside.

3. Spread half of the tomato sauce in a saucepan. Layer half of the eggplant slices, and top with half of the cheddar and mozzarella. Pour half of the ricotta mixture over the layer, or just enough to coat it.

4. Cover the saucepan and insert it into your preheated oven. Bake for 25 minutes. Set to cool for 10 minutes.

5. Repeat the process for the second lasagna set. To serve, garnish your lasagna with chopped parsley

Nutritional Values per Serving:

Calories: 346

Fat: 27g

Protein: 21.4g

Total Carbohydrates: 7.9g

Dietary Fiber: 3.5g

Net Carbohydrates: 4.4g

Beef Broccoli with Sesame Sauce

Serves: 4

Prep Time: 10 minutes

Cooking Time: 45 minutes

Ingredients:

- 2-tbsp coconut oil
- 1-tsp arrowroot powder
- 1-tbsp sesame oil
- 1-tbsp redfish sauce
- ½-tsp light sea salt
- ¼-tsp black pepper
- ¼-tsp baking powder
- 1-lb. beef, sliced into ¼-inch thick chunks
- 2-tsp sesame oil or olive oil
- 1-head broccoli, diced
- 2-tbsp coconut oil
- 2-cloves garlic, minced
- 2-ginger, finely chopped
- A pinch of salt and pepper

Directions:

1. Mix the first seven ingredients in a bowl to make the sesame sauce. Set aside.

2. Fry the meat with sesame oil for 15 minutes until browned.

3. In a saucepan with water, add the broccoli, oil, garlic, and ginger. Season it with a pinch of salt and pepper. Add and spread the fried beef with the broccoli. Cover and cook for 20 minutes. Pour the sauce and cook for 10 more minutes.

Nutritional Values per Serving:

Calories: 375

Fat: 31g

Protein: 19.5g

Total Carbohydrates: 5.4g

Dietary Fiber: 0.8g

Net Carbohydrates: 4.6g

Sautéed Sirloin Steak in Sour Sauce

Serves: 4

Prep Time: 10 minutes

Cooking Time: 30 minutes

Ingredients:

- 1-bulb medium onion, chopped

- 1-clove garlic, minced

- 2-tbsp butter

- 1-lb. sirloin steak, trimmed and cut into thin strips

- ½-tsp salt

- ¼-tsp pepper

- 1-tbsp thyme

- 1½ cup fresh mushrooms, sliced

- 1-tbsp red wine vinegar

- 1-(10.5 oz.) can cream of mushroom soup

- 2-tbsp sour cream

- 4-cups egg noodles, cooked according to package instructions

Directions:

1. Sauté the onion and garlic with melted butter in a large skillet placed over medium heat. Remove from pan and set aside.

2. Add the beef strips, salt, pepper, and thyme. Cook evenly over low heat until browned.

3. Return the onion and garlic, and stir in the mushrooms, wine vinegar, and soup. Cover and simmer for 7 minutes until mushrooms are tender. Uncover and add sour cream. Stir and heat through. Serve immediately over the prepared noodles.

Nutritional Values per Serving:

Calories: 350

Fat: 29.3g

Protein: 17.7g

Total Carbohydrates: 4.9g

Dietary Fiber: 1g

Net Carbohydrates: 3.9g

Flaky Fillets with Garden Greens

Serves: 4

Prep Time: 25 minutes

Cooking Time: 30 minutes

Ingredients:

- 1-lb broccoli, chopped into cubes and seasoned with a dash of salt and pepper

- 2-tbsp coconut oil

- 7-pcs scallions

- 2-tbsp small capers

- 1-tbsp sesame oil or olive oil

- 1½-lbs. white fish, sliced into 4 fillets

- 1-tbsp dried parsley

- 1¼-cups whipping cream, gluten-free and sugar-free

- 1-tbsp mustard, sugar-free

- 1-tsp of salt

- ¼-tsp ground black pepper

- ⅓-cup olive oil

- 5-oz.leafy greens

Directions:

1. Sauté the seasoned broccoli with sesame oil in a pan, and add the scallions and capers. Add the fish in the middle of the sautéed greens. Simmer for 15 minutes.

2. Meanwhile, mix the parsley with the whipping cream and mustard. Pour it over the cooked fish and vegetables. Drizzle with a little bit of coconut oil.

3. Return the saucepan on medium heat and cook for an extra 10 minutes.

Nutritional Values per Serving:

Calories: 395

Fat: 33g

Protein: 19.8g

Total Carbohydrates: 8.7g

Dietary Fiber: 3.9g

Net Carbohydrates: 4.8g

Dinner recipes

Pizza Pie with Cheesy Cauliflower Crust

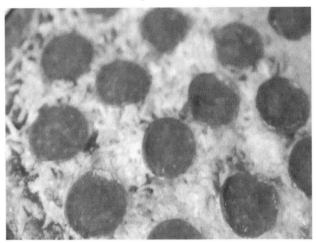

Serves:2

Prep time: 5 minutes

Cooking Time: 30 minutes

Ingredients:

- ½-head cauliflower, rinsed, riced, cooked for 5 minutes in boiling water, and drained

- 2-pcs eggs, whisked

- ⅓-parmesan cheese

- ½-cup cherry tomatoes, washed and halved

- 2-tbsp organic hempseed oil

- 1-tsp balsamic vinegar

- 1-mozzarella cheese ball, crumbled
- ¼-cup basil leaves

Directions:

1. Spin the cooked cauliflower in a dishtowel to let out as much liquid as possible. (The goal is to obtain a flour texture.) Add the eggs and cheese. Mix well.

2. Spread to a disk the cauliflower dough on a baking pan lined with parchment paper. Bake for 15 minutes at 400°F in your preheated oven.

3. Meanwhile, mix the tomatoes with hempseed oil and balsamic vinegar. Season the mixture with salt and pepper.

4. Remove the pizza dough from the oven. Add the tomato mixture and sprinkle over with mozzarella. Return the pan in the oven and bake further for 15 minutes.

5. Serve hot and garnish with fresh basil leaves.

Nutritional Values per Serving:

Calories: 384

Fat: 32.1g

Protein: 19.9g

Total Carbohydrates: 5.5g

Dietary Fiber: 1.7g

Net Carbohydrates: 3.8g

Roasted Rib-eye Skillet Steak

Serves: 2

Prep time: 5 minutes

Cooking Time: 15 minutes

Ingredients:

- 1-16oz rib-eye steak (1 to 1¼-inch thick)

- 2-tbsp duck fat or peanut oil (divided)

- A dash of salt and pepper

- 1-tbsp butter

- ½-tsp thyme, chopped

Directions:

1. Preheat your oven to 400°F. Place a cast iron skillet inside.

2. Season the rib-eye steak with oil, salt, and pepper.

3. Take the preheated skillet out from the oven and place over the stove, set in medium heat. Pour oil, and add the steak. Sear for 2 minutes on both sides.

4. Return the skillet with the steak in the oven. Roast for 6 minutes.

5. Remove the skillet and place over the stove, set in low heat. Add the butter and thyme in the skillet. Baste the steak for about 4 minutes.

Nutritional Values per Serving:

Calories: 722

Fat: 60.2g

Protein: 45g

Total Carbohydrates: 0g

Dietary Fiber: 0g

Net Carbohydrates: 0g

À la Spaghetti with Asian Sauce

Serves: 2

Prep time: 10 minutes

Cooking Time: 15 minutes

Ingredients:

For the Sauce:

- 2-tbsp soy sauce, gluten-free

- 1-tsp of hemp oil

- 1-tsp of lemon juice

- 1-tbsp peanut butter

For the Spaghetti:

- ½-bulb onion, diced

- 1-tsp coconut oil

- 1-tsp red or green pepper, diced

- 1-pc carrot, thinly sliced lengthwise

- 1 egg, whisked

- 5-oz. low-carb spaghetti, rinsed and cooked for 2 minutes in boiling water

- Fresh coriander and peanuts for garnish

Directions:

1. Combine all the sauce ingredients in a bowl. Set aside.

2. Sauté the onion with oil, and add the peppers, carrots, egg, sauce, and spaghetti. Cook for 13 minutes, stirring frequently.

3. To serve, garnish with fresh coriander and peanuts.

Nutritional Values per Serving:

Calories: 412

Fat: 34.4g

Protein: 20.9g

Total Carbohydrates: 10.5g

Dietary Fiber: 5.7g

Net Carbohydrates: 4.8g

Shirataki & Soy Sprouts Pad Thai with Peanut Tidbits

Serves:1

Prep time: 10 minutes

Cooking Time: 5 minutes

Ingredients:

For the Sauce:

- 1-tbsp peanut butter

- 2-tbsp soy sauce, gluten-free

- ½-lime

- 2-tbsp agave syrup, gluten-free

- ½-tbsp organic turmeric

For the Noodles:

- 1-bag of konjac shirataki noodles, rinsed and cooked for 2 minutes in boiling water

- 1-pc carrot, thinly sliced

- 1-bulb onion, thinly sliced

- ½-cup soy sprouts

- ¼-cup unsalted peanuts

- Some sprigs of fresh coriander

Directions:

1. Combine all the sauce ingredients in a bowl. Set aside.

2. Heat the pasta with a little coconut oil in a frying pan. Pour the sauce and add the coriander. Mix well and cook for 5 minutes.

3. To serve, place in a bowl and garnish with peanuts and coriander sprigs.

Nutritional Values per Serving:

Calories: 423

Fat: 35.2g

Protein: 21g

Total Carbohydrates: 14.9g

Dietary Fiber: 9.6g

Net Carbohydrates: 5.3g

Charred Chicken with Squash Seed Sauce

Serves:1

Prep time: 15 minutes

Cooking Time: 20 minutes

Ingredients:

For the Sauce:

- 2-tbsp white almond puree

- 2-cloves of garlic, finely chopped (divided, for the sauce and chicken marinade)

- ½-tbsp squash seeds

- 1-tbsp barley

- 1-pc fresh basil

For the Marinade:

- 2-branches rosemary, finely chopped

- 1-pc red chili, finely chopped

- 1-pc lemon (keep the zest)

- Pinch of salt and ground black pepper

- 1-tbsp olive oil

- 1-cup chicken breasts, cubed

- 5-bulbs small onions, sliced in quarters

- 5-pcs cherry tomatoes

Directions:

1. Combine and mix all the sauce ingredients in a bowl. Set aside.

2. Mix all the marinade ingredients and let stand for 10 minutes. Thread alternately the onions, meat, and tomatoes into the skewers and grill over a coal fire for 10 minutes on each side. Serve the chicken kebabs with the squash seed sauce.

Nutritional Values per Serving:

Calories: 428

Fat: 35.6g

Protein: 21g

Total Carbohydrates: 16.9g

Dietary Fiber: 11.6g

Net Carbohydrates: 5.3g

Therapeutic Turmeric & Shirataki Soup

Serves: 1

Preparation Time: 10 minutes

Cooking Time: 32 minutes

Ingredients:

- 1-tbsp turmeric powder
- 1-serving chicken-vegetable broth soup
- 3-pcs carrots, sliced into small pieces
- 3-slices ginger
- 1-pack (5-oz.) konjac shirataki noodles
- ¼-lb. chicken breast, sliced into strips

Directions:

1. Simmer all the ingredients over low heat for 30 minutes.
2. Rinse the konjac noodles thoroughly under cold water.
3. Add the noodles to the broth and heat for 2 minutes.

Nutritional Values per Serving:

Calories: 415

Fat: 34.6g

Protein: 21.6g

Total Carbohydrates: 10.1g

Dietary Fiber: 5.7g

Net Carbohydrates: 4.4g

Fresh Fettuccine with Pumpkin Pesto

Serves: 3

Prep Time: 15 minutes

Cooking Time: 2 minutes

Ingredients:

For the Pesto Sauce:

- 1-tbsp olive oil

- 1-tbsp pumpkin seed oil

- ½-tsp pumpkin seeds

- ¼-cup barley

- 1-tbsp lemon juice

- A pinch salt

For the Pasta:

- 1¾-cup zucchini, washed, peeled, and cut into thin noodle strips

- ½-cup cherry tomatoes, washed and cut in half

- 1¼-cup low carb fettuccine

- 1-pc mozzarella cheeseball

- A pinch of pepper

Directions:

1. Combine and mix all the sauce ingredients with 2-tbsp water in a bowl. Set aside.

2. Boil the fettuccine for 1 minute and add the zucchini. Boil further for another minute, and drain.

3. Toss the pasta with the pesto sauce. Season the dish with a pinch of pepper and garnish with tomatoes and mozzarella.

Nutritional Values per Serving:

Calories: 417

Fat: 34.7g

Protein: 20.9g

Total Carbohydrates: 10.5g

Dietary Fiber: 5.3g

Net Carbohydrates: 5.2g

Cheddar Chicken Casserole

Serves: 6

Prep Time: 10 minutes

Cooking Time: 30 minutes

Ingredients:

- 20-oz. chicken breasts

- 2-tbsp olive oil (divided)

- 2-cups broccoli, steamed

- ½-cup sour cream

- ½-cup heavy cream

- 1-oz. pork rinds, crushed

- A dash of salt and pepper

- ½-tsp paprika

- 1-tsp oregano

- 1-cup cheddar cheese, grated

Directions:

1. Preheat your oven to 450°F.

2. Sear the chicken with a tablespoon of olive oil in a pan until it cooks all the way through. Shred the meat in the pan. Add the remaining oil, broccoli, and sour cream.

3. Place and spread evenly the mixture in an 8" x11" pan. Press firmly and drizzle with heavy

cream. Add all the remaining seasonings and top the casserole with the cheese. Place the pan in the oven and bake for 25 minutes until the edges turn brown and start bubbling.

Nutritional Values per Serving:

Calories: 405

Fat: 33.8g

Protein: 22.7g

Total Carbohydrates: 3.6g

Dietary Fiber: 1g

Net Carbohydrates: 2.6g

Zesty Zucchini Pseudo Pasta & Sweet Spanish Onions Overload

Serves: 2

Prep Time: 10 minutes

Cooking Time: 20 minutes

Ingredients:

- 2-tbsp of vegetable oil
- 2-pcs yellow onions or Spanish onions
- 1-tbsp low-sodium soy sauce
- 2-tbsp low-sodium teriyaki sauce
- 1-tbsp sesame seeds

- 4-pcs small zucchinis, sliced into spaghetti strips using a spiral cutter

Directions:

1. Add the vegetable oil, onions, and soy sauce to a saucepan placed over medium heat. Stir in the teriyaki sauce and sesame seeds. Mix well until fully combined.

2. Cook for 10 minutes, stirring frequently until the vegetables turn brown.

3. Add the zucchini pasta and cook for 3 minutes.

4. To serve, transfer the pasta in a serving dish and garnish with chopped parsley.

Nutritional Values per Serving:

Calories: 319

Fat: 25.9g

Protein: 18.1g

Total Carbohydrates: 6.6g

Dietary Fiber: 3.2g

Net Carbohydrates: 3.4g

Soba & Spinach Sprouts

Serves: 2

Prep Time: 15 minutes

Cooking Time: 0 minutes

Ingredients:

- 3-pcs mushrooms, sliced into quarters

- ⅓-cup smoked tofu, sliced into squares

- 1-tbsp coconut oil

- ½-pc green pepper, sliced into strips

- 3-tbsp cashew nuts

- ½- clove garlic

- ½-pc lime, juice

- A dash of salt and pepper

- ¼-cup water (more, as needed)

- ¼-cup soba noodles, cooked according to package instructions

- 1⅓-cup spinach sprouts

- 1-tbsp coconut shavings for garnish

Directions:

1. Fry the mushrooms and tofu with coconut oil in a frying pan until they turn brown. Add the pepper. Set aside.

2. For the sauce, mix cashews with garlic, lime juice, salt, pepper, and a little water.

3. Divide the noodles between two bowls and top with spinach sprouts. Arrange the remaining vegetables on top. Garnish with coconut shavings or avocado slices, sesame seeds, and a slice of lime.

4. To serve, pour over the sauce on each arranged bowl.

Nutritional Values per Serving:

Calories: 355

Fat: 29.6g

Protein: 17.8g

Total Carbohydrates: 8.3g

Dietary Fiber: 3.9g

Net Carbohydrates: 4.4g

Chickpeas & Carrot Consommé

Serves: 2

Prep Time: 10 minutes

Cooking Time: 20 minutes

Ingredients:

- ¼-lb. chickpeas, cooked
- 1-tbsp coconut oil
- 1-clove garlic, minced
- 1-piece ginger, minced
- 1-bulb small onion, finely chopped
- ½-lb. carrots, sliced into small pieces
- 1¼-cup vegetable broth
- A dash of salt and pepper
- ½-cup coconut milk
- 1-tbsp coconut shaving

Directions:

1. Arrange the chickpeas on a plate lined with parchment paper. Sprinkle with salt, curry, and paprika. Spread the spices well and bake for 15 minutes at 350°F.

2. Melt the coconut oil in a saucepan and brown the garlic, ginger, and onion. Add the carrots. Deglaze with vegetable broth and simmer for 15

minutes over medium heat until the carrots cook through.

3. Season to taste with salt, pepper, curry, and paprika. Pour the coconut milk.

4. Mix the soup and garnish with chickpeas and coconut shavings.

Nutritional Values per Serving:

Calories: 460

Fat: 38.2g

Protein: 23.3g

Total Carbohydrates: 10.1g

Dietary Fiber: 4.3g

Net Carbohydrates: 5.8g

Chicken Cauliflower Curry

Serves: 2

Prep Time: 15 minutes

Cooking Time: 30 minutes

Ingredients

- 1-cup vegetable broth
- 1-tbsp curry paste
- ½-cup light coconut milk

- ½-lb chicken breast, cooked and sliced into small pieces
- 1-pc potato, diced
- 1-clove garlic, minced
- ½-bulb onion, finely chopped
- 1-cup cauliflower, diced
- ⅓-cup fresh peas
- Salt and pepper
- ¼-cup goji berries

Directions:

1. Heat the vegetable broth in a wok for 5 minutes. Add the curry paste, coconut milk, meat, potato, garlic, and onion. Cook for 15 minutes.

2. Add the vegetables and cook further for 10 minutes until they are tender. Season the curry with a dash of salt and pepper.

3. To serve, garnish with goji berries.

Nutritional Values per Serving:

Calories: 334

Fat: 27g

Protein: 18.7g

Total Carbohydrates: 8.4g

Dietary Fiber: 4.3g

Net Carbohydrates: 4.1g

Cheesy Cauliflower Mac Munchies

Serves: 2

Prep Time: 20 minutes

Cooking Time: 15 minutes

Ingredients:

- 1-pc medium cauliflower, riced
- 3-tbsp + ½-tsp avocado oil (divided)
- A pinch of sea salt
- A pinch of black pepper
- 1-cup cheddar cheese, shredded
- ¼-cup cream, gluten-free
- ¼-cup almond milk, unsweetened

Directions:

1. Preheat your air fryer to 400°F. Spray the pan with oil.

2. Place the riced cauliflower in the pan and drizzle with the avocado oil. Toss well and season with a pinch each of salt and pepper. Set aside.

3. Heat the cheese, cream, and milk with a little bit of avocado oil in a pot.

4. Pour the cheese mixture over the seasoned cauliflower. Lock the lid of the air fryer and set to cook for 14 minutes.

Nutritional Values per Serving:

Calories: 352

Fat: 27.8g

Protein: 20.9g

Total Carbohydrates: 8.9g

Dietary Fiber: 4.3g

Net Carbohydrates: 4.6g

Sugar Snap Pea Pods with Coco Crunch

Serves: 2

Prep Time: 5 minutes

Cooking Time: 10 minutes

Ingredients:

- 4-tbsp salted butter, gluten-free and dairy-free
- 1-tbsp coconut oil
- ½-cup coconut, unsweetened and shredded
- ⅛-tsp cinnamon
- 1-tbsp rosemary oil
- 9-oz. snap pea pods, trimmed, strings removed, and diced
- A pinch of salt

Directions:

1. In a saucepan, melt the coconut oil with the butter over medium heat. Add the coconut shreds, rosemary oil, and cinnamon. Toss very well until fully incorporated.

2. Add the diced pea pods and mix again. Leave to cook for 8 minutes until the pea pods start to melt.

3. To serve, sprinkle over a pinch of salt.

Nutritional Values per Serving:

Calories: 389

Fat: 31.3g

Protein: 22g

Total Carbohydrates: 7.2g

Dietary Fiber: 2.3g

Net Carbohydrates: 4.9g

Spicy & Smoky Spinach-Set Fish Fillets

Serves: 2

Prep Time: 15 minutes

Cooking Time: 10 minutes

Ingredients:

*   2-pcs halibut meat (11-oz. each), membrane removed and deboned

- 4-cups packed spinach

- Juice of ½-pc lemon

- A pinch of salt and pepper

- A pinch of smoked paprika

- 1-pc sliced lemon

- 1-pc green onions, sliced

- 1-pc red chili, deseeded and thinly sliced

- 1-cup cherry tomatoes, halved

- 2-tbsp avocado oil

Directions:

1. Place the halibut meat over a flat surface. Divide the spinach between them.

2. Lay each halibut meat on each pile of spinach. Squeeze the lemon over each part and season with smoked paprika.

3. Top each fish meat with lemon slices, green onions, chili, and the cherry tomatoes. Pour 1-tbsp of avocado oil over each fish portion.

4. Wrap around each fish meat tightly with foil; arrange them in a baking pan. Cook for 10 mins until the fish turns golden and flaky when forked.

Nutritional Values per Serving:

Calories: 248

Fat: 18.8g

Protein: 15.3g

Total Carbohydrates: 13.2g

Dietary Fiber: 8.9g

Net Carbohydrates: 4.3g

Spicy Shrimps & Sweet Shishito

Serves: 2

Prep Time: 15 minutes

Cooking Time: 15 minutes

Ingredients:

- 2-tbsp canola oil

- A pinch of sea salt

- 1-clove garlic, crushed and finely chopped

- 1-pc red chili pepper, seeded and finely chopped

- 5-oz. whole shishito peppers

- 10-oz. shrimps, jumbo size

- 1-tsp sesame oil

- 2-tbsp low-sodium light soy sauce

- Juice of 1-pc lime

Directions:

1. Preheat your air fryer to 350°F for about 5 minutes. Spray your air fryer pan with canola oil.

2. Add the salt, garlic, and red chili pepper. Mix well until fully combined.

3. Add the shishito peppers; mix thoroughly again. Add the shrimps and drizzle with sesame oil.

4. Place the pan in your air fryer and lock the lid. Cook for about 10 minutes at 400°F

5. Divide the dish equally between three serving bowls. To serve, season each bowl with lime juice and soy sauce.

Nutritional Values per Serving:

Calories: 370

Fat: 28.9g

Protein: 23g

Total Carbohydrates: 7.2g

Dietary Fiber: 2.8g

Net Carbohydrates: 4.4g

Spaghetti-Styled Zesty Zucchini with Guacamole Garnish

Serves: 2

Prep Time: 15 minutes

Cooking Time: 5 minutes

Ingredients:

- 2-pcs medium zucchini, cut into spaghetti strips using a spiral cutter

- 1-tbsp sea salt

- 1-pc large avocado, peeled, pitted, and cut into small pieces

- 1⅓-cup fresh basil, washed, dried and finely chopped

- 2-tbsp lemon juice

- A dash of salt and black pepper

- 1-tbsp coconut oil

- 7-oz. mushrooms, cleaned and cut into slices

- 1-pc pomegranate, seeds extracted

Directions:

1. Season the zucchini strips with sea salt and set aside.

2. Mix the avocado slices, lemon juice, and a dash of salt and pepper. Set aside.

3. Toss lightly the zucchini in a frying pan placed over medium heat. Fry for 4 to 5 minutes in coconut oil. Add the mushrooms and pomegranate seeds.

4. To serve, place the zucchini spaghetti on a plate with the avocado cream in a separate bowl. Garnish with the basil leaves.

Nutritional Values per Serving:

Calories: 381

Fat: 31.8g

Protein: 19g

Total Carbohydrates: 14.3g

Dietary Fiber: 9.5g

Net Carbohydrates: 4.8g

Grain-less Gnocchi in Melted Mozzarella

Serves: 1

Prep Time: 10 minutes

Cooking Time: 15 minutes

Ingredients:

- 2-cups mozzarella, shredded

- ½-tsp garlic powder

- 1-tsp salt

- 3-pcs large egg yolks, whisked (divided)

- ½-cup tomato sauce, gluten-free

Directions:

1. Melt the mozzarella with the garlic powder and salt for 5 minutes in a microwave-safe dish.

2. Pour half of the egg yolks into the mozzarella mixture in a large bowl. Mix until fully combined. Add the remaining egg yolks. Mix thoroughly again until fully incorporated.

3. Divide the mixture into four parts. Roll each part into a long rope over a flat surface. Cut each rope into gnocchi-like pieces, pressing each with a fork.

4. Bring a pan filled with water to a boil. Add the gnocchi dumplings and cook for about 2 minutes.

5. Preheat your air fryer to 350°F. Spray the air fryer pan with cooking oil.

6. Arrange the gnocchi pieces in the air fryer pan. Lock the lid of the air fryer and cook for 10 minutes.

7. To serve, pour the tomato sauce over the gnocchi.

Nutritional Values per Serving:

Calories: 355

Fat: 27.6g

Protein: 22.1g

Total Carbohydrates: 6.5g

Dietary Fiber: 2.1g

Net Carbohydrates: 4.4g

Cauliflower Chao Fan Fried with Pork Pastiche

Serves: 4

Prep Time: 20 minutes

Cooking Time: 15 minutes

Ingredients:

- ½-head medium-sized cauliflower, chopped into small cubes
- 2-pcs eggs
- 2-cloves garlic, chopped
- 2-cups pork belly, cut into thin strips
- 3-pcs green capsicums
- 2-bulbs onions
- 1-tbsp soy sauce, gluten-free
- 1-tsp black sesame seeds
- 1-tbsp spring onion, chopped
- 1-tsp pickled ginger

Directions:

1. Place the chopped cauliflower in your food processor; pulse into smaller granules. Set aside.

2. Whisk the eggs, and swirl in the frying pan. Cook for 3 minutes.

3. Add the pork belly strips and the cauliflower rice. Stir in the onions and soy sauce. Cook for about 10 minutes.

4. To serve, distribute the preparation equally between four serving bowls. Garnish with sesame seeds, spring onions, and pickled ginger.

Nutritional Values per Serving:

Calories: 460

Fat: 35.7g |

Protein: 28.6g

Total Carbohydrates: 8.3g

Dietary Fiber: 2.3g

Net Carbohydrates: 6g

All-Avocado Stuffed with Spicy Beef Bits

Serves: 6

Prep Time: 20 minutes

Cooking Time: 20 minutes

Ingredients:

- 1-lb. ground beef
- 1-tbsp chili powder
- ½-tsp salt

- ¾-tsp cumin
- ½-tsp dried oregano
- ¼-tsp garlic powder
- ¼-tsp onion powder
- 4-oz. tomato sauce, gluten-free
- 3-pcs medium-sized avocados, halved and pitted
- 1-cup cheddar cheese, shredded for garnish
- ¼-cup cherry tomatoes, sliced for garnish
- ¼-cup lettuce, shredded for garnish
- A dash of chopped cilantro for garnish

Directions:

1. Cook the beef with oil and a little water in a pan for 10 minutes, stirring frequently until it turns brown. Stir in the spices and tomato sauce. Cook for another 10 minutes.

2. Load the cooked beef to each halved avocado and top with garnish.

Nutritional Values per Serving:

Calories: 280

Fat: 23.1g

Protein: 14g

Total Carbohydrates: 6.3g

Dietary Fiber: 2.2g

Net Carbohydrates: 4.1g

Snacks

Coconut Candy

Serves: 1

Prep time: 10 minutes

Cooking Time: 0 minutes

Ingredients:

- 2-tbsp coconut butter (or notably known as Coconut Manna)

Directions:

1. Melt the coconut butter at room temperature until it resembles a creamy butter consistency.

2. Spoon out the melted butter into candy molds. Refrigerate for 10 minutes to harden before serving.

Nutritional Values per Serving:

Calories: 204

Fat: 17.2g

Protein: 10.2g

Total Carbohydrates: 3g

Dietary Fiber: 0.8g

Net Carbohydrates: 2.2g

Mozzarella Mound Munchies

Serves: 3

Prep time: 5 minutes

Cooking Time: 6 minutes

Ingredients:

- ⅓-cup panko bread, herb-flavored

- 2-pcs egg whites

- 6-tbsp mozzarella cheese, molded into 2-tbsp balls

- ¼-cup marinara sauce

Directions:

1. Preheat your oven to 425°F.

2. Toast the panko breadcrumbs for 2 minutes, stirring frequently, in a medium skillet placed over medium heat.

3. Transfer the breadcrumbs in a bowl. Add the egg whites into a separate bowl.

4. Dip a cheeseball into the egg and roll in the panko. Place the breaded cheese on a greased baking sheet, and bake for 3 minutes. Repeat the process for the remaining cheese.

5. Heat the marinara sauce in your microwave oven for half a minute. Serve the breaded cheeseball with the sauce

Nutritional Values per Serving:

Calories: 157

Fat: 13.2g

Protein: 5.9g

Total Carbohydrates: 4.8g

Dietary Fiber: 1.1g

Net Carbohydrates: 3.7g

Philadelphia Potato Praline

Serves:2

Prep time: 30 minutes

Cooking Time: 0 minutes

Ingredients:

- ⅓-cup Philadelphia cream cheese
- 1½-cup coconut, unsweetened and shredded
- 1-tbsp butter
- ¼-tsp ground cinnamon
- Sweetener of choice

Directions:

1. Mix all the ingredients apart from ground cinnamon in a bowl. Refrigerate the mixture and allow setting until it hardens.

2. Divide the mixture into 8 and roll each portion into potato shapes. Place them on a sheet of parchment paper.

3. Sprinkle all over with the cinnamon and store in the fridge for a week before serving.

Nutritional Values per Serving:

Calories: 180

Fat: 15.3g

Protein: 8.9g

Total Carbohydrates: 3.2g

Dietary Fiber: 1.5g

Net Carbohydrates: 1.7g

Tasty Turkey Cheese Cylinders

Serves: 1

Prep time: 5 minutes

Cooking Time: 0 minutes

Ingredients:

- 1-oz. turkey, roasted and sliced
- 1-oz. cheese

Directions:

1. Slice the cheese into a long strip, enough to fit the turkey slice.

2. Wrap the turkey slice around the cheese.

Nutritional Values per Serving:

Calories: 162

Fat: 10.9g

Protein: 15.6g

Total Carbohydrates: 3.8g

Dietary Fiber: 0g

Net Carbohydrates: 3.8g

Fried Flaxseed Tortilla Treat

Serves: 3

Prep time: 5 minutes

Cooking Time: 10 minutes

Ingredients:

- 6-shells flaxseed tortillas, sliced into chip-sized cuts
- 3-tbsp olive oil
- A dash of salt and pepper

Directions:

1. Fry the flaxseed chips with olive oil in a large pan placed over medium-high heat. Cook for 10 minutes until the chips become crispy, stirring frequently. Strain the chips and place on a paper towel to drain excess oil.

2. Season with salt and pepper.

Nutritional Values per Serving:

Calories: 36

Fat: 2.8g

Protein: 0.8g

Total Carbohydrates: 2.7g

Dietary Fiber: 0.7g

Net Carbohydrates: 2g

Kingly Kale Crispy Chips

Serves:1

Prep time:4 minutes

Cooking Time: 12 minutes

Ingredients

- 1-bunch large kale, rinsed, drained, and stemless

- 2-tbsp olive oil

- 1-tbsp salt

Directions:

1. Preheat your oven to 350°F.

2. Place the kale in a plastic bag. Pour the oil, and mix well by shaking the bag until coating thoroughly each leaf.

3. Spread the kale onto a baking sheet. Press the leaves flat to obtain an evenly crisped cook for each leaf.

4. Bake for 12 minutes until the edges turn brown while the rest of the kales remain dark green.

5. Sprinkle the salt over the baked kale and serve.

Nutritional Values per Serving:

Ambrosial Avocado Puree Pudding

Serves: 3

Prep Time: 5 minutes

Cooking Time: 0 minutes

Ingredients

- 2-ripe Hass avocados, peeled, pitted and cut into chunks
- 2-tsp organic vanilla extract
- 80-drops of liquid sweetener
- 1-can (113.5-oz.) organic coconut milk
- 1-tbsp lime juice from organic lime

Directions

1. Combine all the ingredients in a blender. Blend to a smooth and velvety consistency. Pour the blend equally between three glasses. Chill before serving.

Nutritional Values per Serving:

Calories: 240

Fat: 23.8g

Protein: 2.8g

Total Carbohydrates: 12.8g

Dietary Fiber: 9g

Net Carbohydrates: 3.8g

Power-Packed Butter Balls

Serves: 5

Prep Time: 80 minutes

Cooking Time: 0 minutes

Ingredients:

- 2-tbsp cocoa powder + 1-tbsp for dusting
- 2-tbsp plain oatmeal, gluten-free
- ⅔-cup peanut butter or chia butter
- 1-tbsp organic chia seeds
- 3-tbsp protein powder

Directions:

1. Mix the cocoa powder, oatmeal, peanut butter chia seeds, and protein powder.
2. By using your hand, form balls from the mixture. Dust each ball with cocoa powder.
3. Place the balls in the fridge for 1 hour before serving.

Nutritional Values per Serving:

Calories: 128

Fat: 10.1g

Protein: 4.9g

Total Carbohydrates: 7.2g

Dietary Fiber: 2.9g

Net Carbohydrates: 4.3g

Choco Coco Cups

Serves: 10

Prep Time: 50 minutes

Cooking Time: 0 minutes

Ingredients:

For the Coconut Base:

- ½-cup coconut butter

- ½-cup coconut oil

- ½-cup unsweetened coconut, shredded

- 3-tbsp powdered sweetener

For the Chocolate Topping:

- 3-oz. sugar-free dark chocolate

Directions:

1. Line a muffin pan with 20 mini parchment cups.

2. Heat the coconut butter with the coconut oil in a saucepan placed over low heat. Stir until the butter melts. Stir in the sweetener and coconut and sweetener until fully combined.

3. Divide the mixture equally between the prepared muffin cups. Freeze for 30 minutes until firm.

4. Melt the dark chocolate and spoon over the cold filling. Let it sit for 15 minutes before serving.

Nutritional Values per Serving:

Calories: 240

Fat: 25.3g

Protein: 2.1g

Total Carbohydrates: 5g

Dietary Fiber: 4g

Net Carbohydrates: 1g

Corndog Clumps

Serves: 10

Prep Time: 5 minutes

Cooking Time: 15 minutes

Ingredients:

- ¼-tsp. baking powder
- ¼-tsp. salt
- ½-cup almond flour
- ½-cup flaxseed meal
- 1-tbsp psyllium husk powder
- 3-packets sweetener
- 1-pc large egg

- ⅓-cup sour cream

- ¼-cup melted butter

- ¼-cup coconut milk

- 10-pcs (2-oz.) smoked sausage, sliced in half

Directions:

1. Preheat your oven to 375°F. Grease a 20-cup muffin pan.

2. Combine the first six ingredients in a bowl. Add the egg, sour cream, and butter and mix well. Pour in the coconut milk, and mix again. Pour the batter in the pan.

3. Insert a sliced sausage into the center of each muffin. Place the pan in the oven.

4. Bake for 12 minutes; thereafter, broil for 3 minutes, set on high heat.

Nutritional Values per Serving:

Calories: 148

Fat: 13.2g

Protein: 3.9g

Total Carbohydrates: 4g

Dietary Fiber: 1.6g

Net Carbohydrates: 3.4g

Desserts

Cool Cucumber Sushi with Sriracha Sauce

Serves:4

Prep time: 20 minutes

Cooking Time: 0 minutes

Ingredients:

For the Sushi:

- 2-pcs medium cucumbers

- ¼-pc avocado, thinly sliced

- 2-pcs small carrots, thinly sliced

- ½-pc red bell pepper, thinly sliced

- ½-pc yellow bell pepper, thinly sliced

For the Sriracha Sauce:

- ⅓-cup mayonnaise

- 1-tbsp sriracha

- 1-tsp soy sauce, gluten-free

Directions:

1. Slice one end of the cucumbers, and core them by using a small spoon to remove the seeds until completely hollow.

2. By using a butter knife, press the avocado slices into the center of each cucumber. Slide in the carrots and bell peppers until filling up completely each cucumber.

3. To make the dipping sauce, whisk to combine all the sauce ingredients in a bowl.

4. Slice the cucumber into 1"-thick round pieces, Serve with sauce on the side.

Nutritional Values per Serving:

Calories: 110

Fat: 10.1g

Protein: 1.9g

Total Carbohydrates: 4.8g

Dietary Fiber: 2g

Net Carbohydrates: 2.8g

Coco Crack Bake-less Biscuit Bars

Serves:6

Prep time: 2 minutes

Cooking Time: 3 minutes

Ingredients:

- 3-cups unsweetened coconut flakes, shredded

- 1-cup coconut oil, melted

- ¼-cup liquid sweetener of choice

Directions:

1. Line an 8"-square baking pan with parchment paper. Set aside.

2. Combine all the ingredients in a large mixing bowl. Mix well to a thick batter. (Add a little liquid sweetener or water if the batter is too crumbly.

3. Pour and press firmly the mixture in the prepared pan. Refrigerate until firm.

4. To serve, slice the hardened mixture into 2" x 8" bars.

Nutritional Values per Serving:

Calories: 106

Fat: 10.5g

Protein: 2.9g

Total Carbohydrates: 2g

Dietary Fiber: 2g

Net Carbohydrates: 0g

Chocolate-Coated Sweet Strawberries

Serves: 8

Prep time:3 hours 5 minutes

Cooking Time: 0 minutes

Ingredients:

- 2-cups melted chocolate chips, dairy-free

- 2-tbsp coconut oil

- 16-pcs fresh strawberries, with stems

Directions:

1. Combine the melted chocolate and coconut oil in a medium bowl. Mix well until fully combined.

2. Scoop the chocolate mixture into each mold of an ice cube tray. Top each with strawberry, with its stem part up. Pour the remaining chocolate mixture over strawberries. Freeze for at least 3 hours until the chocolate hardens.

Nutritional Values per Serving:

Calories: 125

Fat: 11.1g

Protein: 2.7g

Total Carbohydrates: 5g

Dietary Fiber: 1.4g

Net Carbohydrates: 3.6g

Matcha Muffins with Choco-Coco Coating

Serves:4

Prep time: 15 minutes

Cooking Time: 15 minutes

Ingredients:

- ½-cup almond flour

- 1-tbsp yeast

- 1-tbsp cooking matcha powder

- 1-tbsp cashew nuts

- ½-cup milk substitute with hydrogenated vegetable oil

- 1-tbsp peanut butter

- 1-tbsp cacao nibs

- 1-tbsp coconut syrup, gluten-free

- 3-tbsp milk substitute with hydrogenated vegetable oil

- A handful of Goji berries (or blueberries and raspberries) and cocoa nuggets (optional)

Directions:

1. Mix the flour, yeast, matcha powder, cashews. Pour ½-cup of vegetable milk gradually while mixing into the dough.

2. Put the dough in a pre-greased muffin pan. Bake for 15 minutes at 350°F.

3. Mix the peanut butter with cacao, syrup, and milk to make the icing. To serve, pour the icing and garnish with cocoa nuggets and Goji berries.

Nutritional Values per Serving:

Calories: 140

Fat: 10.9g

Protein: 5.1g

Total Carbohydrates: 8.8g

Dietary Fiber: 3.4g

Net Carbohydrates: 5.4g

Cinnamon Cup Cake

Serves: 1

Prep Time: 1 minute

Cooking Time: 0 minutes

Ingredients:

- 1-scoop vanilla protein powder
- ½-tsp baking powder
- 1-tbsp coconut flour
- ½-tsp cinnamon
- 1-tbsp granulated sweetener of choice
- ¼-cup almond milk
- ¼-tsp vanilla extract
- 1-tsp granulated sweetener of choice
- ½-tsp cinnamon powder

For the Butter Glaze:

- 1-tbsp coconut butter, melted
- ½-tsp almond milk
- A pinch of cinnamon powder

Directions:

1. Combine the protein powder, baking powder, coconut flour, cinnamon, and sweetener in a

greased microwave-safe bowl. Mix well until fully combined.

2. Pour the milk, vanilla extract, and sweetener. Mix thoroughly to form a batter. (Add some milk if the batter is too crumbly). Top with a sprinkling of cinnamon powder.

3. Cook in the microwave for 1-minute. Meanwhile, combine all the butter glaze ingredients in a bowl. To serve, top the cake with the butter glaze.

Nutritional Values per Serving:

Calories: 263

Fat: 24.1g

Protein: 7.6g

Total Carbohydrates: 14.2g

Dietary Fiber: 10.3g

Net Carbohydrates: 3.9g

Choco 'Cado Twin Truffles

Serves: 5

Prep Time: 30 minutes

Cooking Time: 0 minutes

Ingredients:

- 1-cup melted dark chocolate chips, dairy-free

- 1-pc small avocado, mashed

- 1-tsp vanilla extract

- ¼-tsp kosher salt

- ¼-cup cocoa powder

Directions:

1. Combine the melted chocolate with avocado, vanilla, and salt in a bowl. Mix well until fully combined. Refrigerate for 20 minutes to firm up slightly.

2. By using a small spoon, scoop about a tablespoon of the chocolate mixture and roll it on the palm of your hand's palm to form a ball. Repeat the process to consume the mixture.

3. Roll each ball in cocoa powder.

Nutritional Values per Serving:

Calories: 68

Fat: 5.8g

Protein: 1.6g

Total Carbohydrates: 4.2g

Dietary Fiber: 1.8g

Net Carbohydrates: 2.4g

Butter Ball Bombs

Serves: 10

Prep Time: 65mins

Cooking Time: 0 minutes

Ingredients:

- 8-tbsp (1 stick) butter, softened to room temperature
- ⅓-cup sweetener
- ½-teaspoon. pure vanilla extract
- ½-teaspoon. kosher salt
- 2-cups almond flour
- ⅔-cup unsweetened dark chocolate chips, dairy-free

Directions:

1. Use your hand mixer and beat the butter in a large bowl until light and fluffy. Add the vanilla extract, sweetener, and salt. Beat again until fully combined.

2. Add gradually the almond flour, beating continuously until no dry portions remain. Fold in the chocolate chips. Cover the bowl with a plastic wrap and refrigerate for 20 minutes to firm slightly.

3. By using a small spoon, scoop the dough to form into small balls.

Nutritional Values per Serving:

Calories: 51

Fat: 4.3g

Protein: 0.7g

Total Carbohydrates: 2.7g

Dietary Fiber: 0.4g

Net Carbohydrates: 2.3g

Choco Coco Cookies

Serves: 6

Prep Time: 10 minutes

Cooking Time: 15 minutes

Ingredients:

- ¼-cup coconut oil
- 4-pcs egg yolks
- 2-tablespoon sweetener
- 1-cup dark unsweetened chocolate chips
- 1-cup coconut flakes
- 4-tablespoon butter, softened
- ¾-cup walnuts,chopped roughly

Directions:

1. Preheat your oven to 350°F. Use a parchment paper to line a baking tray.

2. Mix all the ingredients in a large mixing bowl until fully combined.

3. Form cookies out of the mixture, and place them in the baking tray. Bake for 15 minutes until golden.

4. Serve and enjoy.

Nutritional Values per Serving:

Calories: 130

Fat: 11.5g

Protein: 2.9g

Total Carbohydrates: 6g

Dietary Fiber: 2.2g

Net Carbohydrates: 3.8g

Carrot Compact Cake

Serves: 8

Prep Time: 20 minutes

Cooking Time: 0 minutes

Ingredients:

- 1-block (8-oz.) cream cheese, softened

- ¾-cup coconut flour
- 1-teaspoon sweetener
- ½-teaspoon pure vanilla extract
- 1-teaspoon cinnamon
- ¼-teaspoon ground nutmeg
- 1-cup carrots, grated
- 1-cup unsweetened coconut, shredded
- ½-cup pecans, chopped

Directions:

1. Mix the first six ingredients in a large mixing bowl. Mix well by using a hand mixer until fully combined. Fold in the pecans and carrots.

2. Form 16 balls from the mixture, and roll each ball in shredded coconut.

Nutritional Values per Serving:

Calories: 94

Fat: 8.3g

Protein: 2.8g

Total Carbohydrates: 5.2g

Dietary Fiber: 3.1g

Net Carbohydrates: 2.1g

Chilled Cream

Serves: 8

Prep Time: 8 hours 15 minutes

Cooking Time: 0 minutes

Ingredients:

- 2-cans (15-oz.) coconut milk, refrigerated for at least 3 hours

- 2-cups heavy cream

- 1-teaspoon pure vanilla extract

- ¼-cup sweetener

- A pinch of kosher salt

Directions:

1. Spoon the refrigerated coconut milk into a large bowl. Leave the liquid in the can. By using a hand mixer, beat the milk until turning creamy. Set aside.

2. Beat the heavy cream in a separate large bowl until it forms soft peaks. Add the vanilla and sweetener. Beat again until fully combined.

3. Fold in the whipped milk into the whipped cream. Mix well and transfer the mixture in a loaf pan.

4. Place the pan in the freezer for 5 hours until the mixture becomes solid.

Nutritional Values per Serving:

Calories: 340

Fat: 34.8g

Protein: 3.7g

Total Carbohydrates: 5.2g

Dietary Fiber: 2.1g

Net Carbohydrates: 3.1g

Conclusion

Thank you for taking your time to download the book "Intermittent Fasting 16/8: Complete Step-By-Step Guide to Lose Weight Quickly, Control Hunger and Feel Better Without Sacrificing Your Favorite Foods. Included: Meal Plans with Delicious Recipes".

Many people struggle with dieting plans and getting one that's capable of providing the desired results has always been a challenge. One thing that makes Intermittent fasting to be significant is the fact that fasting is a practice that comes so naturally to the body. It's easy to start fasting and flexible to sustain as you don't have to worry about the foods that you eat and the macronutrients.

I know that you have found valuable information regarding what 16:8 Intermittent fasting entails and how you can make use of it for optimal health and weight loss. Intermittent fasting doesn't have to be a struggle if you choose the right fasting protocol that suits you best and goes by the guidelines.

It's important to note that intermittent fasting is not a quick fix; you will not automatically lose weight just because you are fasting. You also have to watch your diet and ensure that the foods that you consume are helping you towards realizing your desired goal.

Thanks for choosing this book, make sure to leave a short review on Amazon if you enjoy it, I'd really love to hear your thoughts!